ENERGY IN MOTION

How to Unleash Your Mind and Take Action Now

Alejandra Díaz Mercado

Energy in Motion: How To Unleash Your Mind and Take Action Now
www.energyinmotionbook.com

Copyright © 2020 Alejandra Díaz Mercado

ISBN: 978-1-77277-3934

All rights reserved. No portion of this book may be reproduced mechanically, electronically, or by any other means, including photocopying, without permission of the publisher or author except in the case of brief quotations embodied in critical articles and reviews. It is illegal to copy this book, post it to a website, or distribute it by any other means without permission from the publisher or author.

Limits of Liability and Disclaimer of Warranty
The author and publisher shall not be liable for your misuse of the enclosed material. This book is strictly for informational and educational purposes only.

Warning – Disclaimer
The purpose of this book is to educate and entertain. The author and/or publisher do not guarantee that anyone following these techniques, suggestions, tips, ideas, or strategies will become successful. The author and/or publisher shall have neither liability nor responsibility to anyone with respect to any loss or damage caused, or alleged to be caused, directly or indirectly by the information contained in this book.

Medical Disclaimer
The medical or health information in this book is provided as an information resource only, and is not to be used or relied on for any diagnostic or treatment purposes. This information is not intended to be patient education, does not create any patient-physician relationship, and should not be used as a substitute for professional diagnosis and treatment.

Publisher
10-10-10 Publishing
Markham, ON Canada

Printed in Canada and the United States of America

Table of Contents

Foreword xi
Acknowledgements xiii

Chapter 1: In the Beginning There Was … 1
Certainties 3
Change 5
Tomatoes 7
Darkness... 10
In Light of Awareness 12

Chapter 2: Mind Games 17
How to Short-Circuit Your Brain.. 19
Brain Is not Mind... 21
Broken Minds... 25
The Unconscious Mind 29
Beware of the Dog 32

Chapter 3: Secrets of Successful Shapeshifters 34
Shapeshifting for Beginners.. 37
Growth in Threes 40
Coachability and Teachability Cups 41
Being at Cause 43
Yes I Do… 45

Chapter 4: The Fabric of Reality 47
Self-Fulfilling Prophecies 49
If You Hate a Cat 51
How to Sleep Better at Night..52
Let's Agree to Disagree 54
The Ego Self 57

Chapter 5: Digesting Reality...61
The All-You-Can-Eat Reality Buffet 63
How to Eat Cake 66
This Is Fruit Loops..68
Mind Your Mouth...69
Self-Hypnosis..72

Chapter 6: Energy in Motion 77
The Ignition Key 79
To Embody the Force..81
Emotions 83
Source and Purpose 87
Emotional Vibes..89

Chapter 7: The Art of Swimming in the Dark........................93
Understanding the Purpose of Negative Emotions 95
The Unwarranted and the Purposeful 97
Wild Creatures of the Deep Dark..101
The Superpower of Empathy 105
The Illusion of Drowning in a Glass of Water................................107

Chapter 8: Human Problems 111
Good Apple, Bad Apple: Judging Thoughts 113
Crabs in a Bucket: What Happens When You Change?.................116
The Chocolate or Vanilla Curse, Courtesy of Your Power
   of Choice 119
The Power to Procrastinate 121
Destructive Abundance and Our Demise from Paradise 124

Chapter 9: The Blueprint to Higher Consciousness 129
The Golden Ratio and the God of Math..131
Highs, Lows, and Flows..133
Breakdowns and Breakthroughs 137
The Dark Night of the Soul 139
COVID-19 and the Breakdown of the Self 140
Consciousness Expands in Breakdowns 143

Chapter 10: How to Unleash Your Mind 149
The Responsibility of Human Consciousness 151
The Three Tests of a Hero 152
Your Soul Map..157
How to Take Back Personal Power 160
Creating Vibrational Coherence...163
Exercise Your Power to Create 168
This Is My Blank Page..171

About the Author 173

What is this spark
that ignites motion,
The flame that follows
and, uncontrolled,
The overwhelming wildfire
that consumes us.

*To my husband, Omar Arvizu,
the genius who mentored the understanding
of my body as a vehicle of movement;
the lover who has never attempted to
tame the wild horses of my madness;
the guardian who keeps me grounded
while I explore the stars.*

FOREWORD

It is not by chance that you have this book in your hands. You are meant to have it and you are meant to read it.

However it happened for you to now be reading these words, know that you are standing at the apex of infinite possibilities, all converging in this very moment. As a result of what you have been thinking, feeling, speaking and doing, you have attracted this book into your hands. You most commonly know this phenomenon as the *Law of Cause and Effect* or the *Law of Attraction*.

The book itself carries a series of code words designed to create contrast, and it will either attract or repel you. You may not be ready to move physically, emotionally, mentally, or to step into more personal power.

Stepping into more of your personal power comes along with taking responsibility for how you think, feel, speak and behave. With *Energy in Motion: How to Unleash your Mind and Take Action Now,* Alejandra has done a masterful job of creating a stepping stone for you, if you are ready to take that responsibility.

Whether you *feel* ready or not, this book will guide you while you journey into obscure aspects of your psyche. It is your birthright to bring into conscious awareness how you are made and what your true potential is. It is also your birthright to choose whether you want to act on it or not, but you cannot truly know if you are ready unless you know what ready means.

Alejandra is a visionary when it comes to bridging some of the language gaps that could potentially be limiting your ever-expanding experience of being human. A *coincidence* is an isolated experience that turns into a complex and interconnected *synchronicity* when you realize the extent of the causes involved in any given incident. The experience of expanding in consciousness and living up to your potential as a human being arises from the integration of concepts, not from separation. If you are open to it, this book will provide mind sparking content for you to discover what integration means in your world.

I first met Alejandra at an event where she performed as a kinetic artist. Later that same year, I had the pleasure of working with her to bring about the creation of *Energy in Motion* and I thought to myself, who else could bring about such an insightful book than she who indeed embodies the meaning of energy in motion?!

As her publisher I am proud and pleased to watch this insightful woman finally complete her newest work of art. I have a feeling the treasures contained within these pages will serve as a beacon of light for you, if you are looking to live up to your true potential on this planet.

Raymond Aaron
New York Times Bestselling Author

ACKNOWLEDGEMENTS

To those who assist me in my understanding of my soul and the world around me, I thank you and honor you because YOU are part of my journey, and it is my wish that this book will accompany you and assist you in yours.

EXPANDING MY SOUL

First and foremost, I thank my husband, **Omar Arvizu**, who has surpassed the earthly concept of *husband* and turned himself into a *super husband* for me. He seems to be an unlimited source of love and caring for me, and it is thanks to the way he loves and cares for me that I can put my wholehearted focus into the act of creation in various realms of my life. I am awed at how easily he loves the light and the darkness that is me, without any judgement. Even though he has self-proclaimed that his first job is to take care of me, he still finds time and energy to nurture our home, inspire his movement clients, renovate houses, and has even reinvented himself into a new career. He awed me with his patience while I was writing this book, especially when I wouldn't stop talking about concepts that didn't seem to make sense, and then took over his computer, the two tablets we have at home, the bedroom, the dining table and the couch, with notes and maps for my book, even though I have a full studio for myself. It wasn't always fun when he pushed me to finish my book—sometimes he bribed me with coffee, and other times with sarcasm—but he was there every step of the way. He is my guardian angel. I love you, Omar Arvizu.

I am thankful and blessed to have **Rodrigo Díaz Mercado** as my little brother in this lifetime. He is like another slice of my soul that helps me see beyond my self-righteous views. It was just about a year ago when he stepped through the door into the world of quantum chats, awareness of energy, the art of manifesting, downloads, and awakenings. It was then that we became partners in crime and vowed to each other to write our own books. As he fulfilled his quest before me, my little brother became my big brother who now inspires me. We had endless morning calls and family visits where our mouths wouldn't stop conversing, discussing, creating contrast, and defining the concepts that he and I wanted to share with the world. As where I represent chaos, cynicism, and often swim in darkness, he is the light of compassion in my life. He reminds me that being naive also means staying hopeful and magical in a world full of personal turmoil.

I am blessed to have **Perla Chávez** as my mother, my gateway and guide to life. She loved me and nurtured me in mind, body, and spirit, and kept my world safe and perfect, allowing me to bloom undisturbed into the blessed adult that I am today. I know she made personal sacrifices and fought battles to defend me. I learned to be a warrior woman by seeing the warrior in her. She represents strength and balance in my life, with a work ethic that few could ever match, and her commitment to health with space for a sweet afternoon treat that she would always share with me. Her life wisdom is entwined in the pages of this book as well, so that she may live forever.

Another blessing in my life is to have **Alejandro Díaz Mercado** as my father. I have always felt foreign in this world, as if I had come from another planet, but he made me his favorite human and became the superhero who has always taken care of me. He kept my world full of magic and adventure by partaking in my love for fantasy and showing me the magic native to this world: NATURE. My father represents charisma in my world. I was always awed by watching him embody energy in motion as a physical education teacher and a camp director. When he spoke, when he sang, when he told stories, hundreds of children and dozens of adults would gather around him. They would have followed him to the end of the world. His wisdom is also embedded in these pages, so that he may live forever.

I thank, with all my heart, **Allison Woodley**, who came into my family and became my little sister. She taught me that strength doesn't always need to be loud, and that wisdom can be built in silence. I have watched her transform the odds and transmute matter. I am watching her and becoming awed by the speed of her growth and the ripple effect she has begun. She represents compassion, kindness, and childlike wonder in my world.

UNDERSTANDING OF MY INNER AND OUTER WORLDS

I am blessed with the presence of **Michelle Labrosse** in my world, whose belief in me continues to transmute the very essence of who I am. I am moved and awed by her commitment to a cruelty-free world, and by the courageous actions she takes day after day as a vegan activist to be a voice for those who don't have a voice or a choice. A peaceful warrior, Michelle is the embodiment of energy in motion that transforms this world. Thank you for the gift of sharing your life and your passions with me.

To my dear friend, **Rob Muir**, among all the energy that moves in my world, I still have a need for a solid wall. Among all the people that come and go, you have remained, and among all the shapeshifting that I have done since we met, you still remain. I do not need to fear you will disappear, like a lot of things have disappeared in my life. You represent a calm permanence and good judgement in my world. Thank you for the gift of your friendship in my life, because certain things indeed come and go, but your friendship remains.

A special thank you to **Brendan Coates** because, as time went by, and many forgot I was writing a book, including myself, you came with a firm hand and a firm voice to disrupt the delusion I had trapped myself in. You re-ignited the energy I needed to finish this book. I am thankful for your presence in my world, as you represent health and wisdom of the body and mind, and you embody the wholehearted commitment that a soul on a mission needs in order to fulfill its life's purpose.

I am thankful for the presence of **Jeff Morrison** in my world. Your interest in my words and my book intrigued me and fueled me to move past a personal block. Your calm exterior holds the gift of attentiveness and kindness that shines from your heart and into important aspects of my world. Thank you for the gift of your friendship in my life.

I am blessed to have **Kirsten Frey** as an awakened friend and guide. The work she did with me to understand and navigate grief is unlike anything I have encountered before. With the heart of a sage and the strength of a warrior she stood with me as we journeyed through darkness, and I came out with a new understanding of grief as part of the human experience. Thank you.

I am grateful for the friendship with **Josh Seraj,** and the challenge he presented me the moment he unleashed on me the question of what would I leave behind after I died. A loaded question indeed, but only someone so close to me could have delivered such a daring statement with the impact it had. Josh, this book is part of my legacy. If you have this in your hands I have the certainty that I will not disappear in the failing memories of those who have known me.

I thank **Raymond Aaron,** my publisher, for being a powerful creator and, with his creations, enabling me to step into more of my personal power, providing the tools necessary for me to bring ideas from the spirit world into manifested reality. You turned my world upside down, and it was then that I saw the missing pieces. When I came back from this adventure, I was built anew, and I became a powerful creator.

DISCOVERING MY BODY AS A VEHICLE TO TRANSMUTE MY WORLD

I am very thankful for the presence of **Mike Fitch** in my life, and for the opportunities I have had to evolve my Animal Flow practice, learning directly from him, the source. Mike, creator and president of Animal Flow, has gifted the world with a discipline that has the potential to transcend space, time, and language, and create meaningful connections with people from all over the world. This has been my experience with this practice, which became part of my life in 2015. Animal Flow enables me to embody energy in motion and continuously transcend my own physical and mental limitations. I thank Mike for his gift in my world. Thank you for being a daring creator, a movement artist, and a sound scientist. Thank you for your support in bringing energy to the completion of this book.

A special thank you to **Karen Mahar**, COO of Animal Flow. Meeting you had a powerful entrepreneurial impact on me, as I became aware of how important your role is as an architect behind the systems that run Animal Flow. You made me aware of the architectural order I needed to develop behind the artist in me, if my mission is indeed to share something meaningful with the world. Thank you, Karen, for the wonderful experience you allowed me to have at the Animal Flow Level 2 retreat in 2019. It changed me forever, and it gives me something to look forward to every year.

It was also there that I met **Venus Lau, Victor Reyes, Andrea Zylinsky, Caroline Taylor, Guillaume Tual, Kathryn West, Rachel Thompson, Roshan Chopra** and **Sui Wong** in person, and every day I continue to rejoice in meeting more inspiring and powerful individuals from my Animal Flow family. You are the embodiment of energy in motion in my world. I am awed and comforted to know that you are part of this powerful energy that moves me, and this kind of magic is sprinkled all over the world. May we see each other again soon!

A heartfelt thank you to **Fréyja Spence** and **Dain Wallis** creators of Move Daily for providing a space for me in their home project to share my voice with the world. Fréyja, who also coached my initiation in Animal Flow, was the first person who explained to me some of the mysteries of hypermobility within my body and helped me understand how to manage it as a superpower rather than fighting it as a weakness.

I am so grateful to have the presence of **Sean Everingham,** creator and president of Ultimate Fitness Shows, in my life. The mission and values that his association stands for enabled one of the most self-fulfilling experiences I have ever had on stage as a bodybuilder. After having competed nine other times with different associations, it wasn't until I set foot on the UFE stage that I felt true to myself, and I could fully unleash all that is within me as a bodybuilder and movement artist. I am grateful for the gift you gave me to finally be myself on stage. I admire your creation and the values it stands for, and I am proud to be a **UFE Pro**.

A heartfelt thank you to **Sean Tierney** for having the vision to harness my work ethic and commitment to being the best expression of my physical self, and giving me the map to understand the discipline and art of bodybuilding. For more than 10 years, this continues to be a pillar in the construction of my body and world.

I want to thank **Anita Kus-Roberts** for igniting the physical transformation that completely changed the course of my future. I believe that the beginning of this book took root in *that* October of 2010.

THE MEANING OF THE WORLD AROUND ME

The presence of the warrior force of **Joe Arko** manifested itself in my world at a moment where I needed to re-calibrate my course. When I went to war with myself during COVID-19, I didn't go at it alone. I had the firm hand, support, and guidance of Joe. It wasn't always fun when he tested my boundaries, but that is what a warrior guide does. Thank you for the gift of your indomitable strength and the vision to be a pathfinder in my world.

A special thank you to **Sara Fennell** for being the presence of a powerful female entrepreneur in my life, an intuitive creator and guide who helped me evolve in my understanding of who I needed to become in the online world so that my message could be heard.

Thank you **Joe Arko, Sara Fennell, Teresa Heron, Justin D'Olimpio, Lydia Di Francesco, Ema Suvajac, Jodi Boam, Rosie Metayer, Bharat Oza, Ken Sylvan, Claudia Baillargeon, Alissa Blais,** and **David Blais** for the space, time, and attention you gifted me at the Mastermind, during a time when I did not know where I was headed, and my energy was in idle mode. Your trust, your courage, your insights, and what you shared with me during our time together, were the gentle nudge I needed to move forward into my new self. Thank you.

I am thankful to have had **Lindsay Boardman** as a mentor in my early career as a movement coach. She is a powerful creator and a business visionary, and she is personable, kind, and giving, with an exceptional sense of humor. Her qualities as my guide are in big part the reason why I took off very successfully early in my career as a personal trainer and business entrepreneur, and continue to be a successful business woman within the fitness world. Thank you for the early years of guidance, and thank you for the later years of friendship. As a powerful creator, thank you for Meraki Fitness, and for putting your heart and soul into a place I also call my home.

Meraki Fitness is where I have had the gift of reuniting with **Alison Wiseman, Laura Wolfe, Stephanie Caetano,** and **Nicola Folino,** and the gift of getting to know **Derek Knight, Joey Nemet, Cassandra Belle, Adrienne Lee, Karen Forrester, Alena Luciani, Bryan Chang, Damon Edwards, Taylor Patterson,** and **Marcas Patrick.** Know that however short or long our interactions were, you and your presence at Meraki brought a spark to my weird introverted self.

Another blessing in my life is **Alana Connell.** As a mentor later in my career, she gifted me with her personal belief in me, reigniting my spark, which took me to new and unprecedented heights in my personal training career with GoodLife Fitness. That year, under her guidance, not only did I compete internationally as a bodybuilder, winning 4th place at The Arnolds Amateurs in the USA, I also won a Canada-wide company award, a feat that the general consensus deemed impossible. Your unwavering belief in me fueled me. What a year! Later on, her light guided me as I stepped into the uncharted territory of reinventing myself within the company and without the company. Thank you for the gift of Barbella Studio, and thank you for the gift of your light and your friendship.

I wholeheartedly thank **Suzanne Longstreet**, my Master NLP Coach and Trainer, for her presence in my life and her power in this world; for her fire, her courage, her leadership, and her passion and compassion as my guide. Suzanne is the guide I had been waiting for all my life. In my understanding of the Universe and the world inside myself, there is such a thing as before and after Suzanne. Suzanne brought integration and cohesion to my inner world, and assisted me in clearing my mind and my soul so that I could share my gifts with the world. It is thanks to Suzanne that I have the courage to take a stand for myself and others, to create a safe space to understand darkness, speak with demons and reignite the passion for living a powerful human life.

I did not achieve my Neuro-linguistic Programming Master Practitioner status by myself. I want to thank and acknowledge the light and courage of the women who traversed uncharted territory with me, and whose experiences changed me as well: **Celine Roy-Higgins, Ida Tetlock, Sandi Hettrick Browne, Lisa Reaume, Julie Creighton, Tracy Grant, Liz Zelko, Cheryl Spalding, Gina Bello, Anna S. Hill,** and **Cara Melo,** who to me is a fascinating force of nature with whom I unexpectedly struck a friendship during transition times, and who has been a blessing in my life.

I am thankful for the presence of **Eric Wong Kai Pun** in my life, who has always known that I was a unicorn in a world full of horses, and who had the vision to gift me with a word, a piece of advice, a phone call or a book with synchronic resonance to what I needed at that moment in time. I appreciate you and the mad genius of your mind. I am thankful for the challenges and the learnings you brought my way.

I am grateful to have met **Ilana MacDonald,** a woman of such professionalism, strength, and certainty that infused me with the focus I needed to outdo myself and shine in a world where I felt I didn't belong. Thank you for guiding me and believing in me.

I am also grateful for the direction I received from **Ryan Donnelly** during this pivotal time in my career. His support and undying belief in me were a light during dark times. I am grateful for the open door you still hold for me.

TO THOSE WHO COMPLETE MY WORLD

Pey Ferrando, Kristin O'Brien, Eden Esposo, Andrew James, Michelle Labrosse, and **Omar Arvizu,** thank you for accepting my ludicrous offer to be my zombie. Thank you for the courage and strength it took from you to make it until the end of this project, and thank you for the days, the time, and energy that you gifted me in this quest to jump on stage. Those memories, I will treasure forever. You and I created that moment in time together to embody this artistic aspect of energy in motion in my world. You are part of my world.

Pey Ferrando, I thank you for coming from a very distant land. May this book accompany you in all your own energy in motion studies and adventures as a warrior, shapeshifter, mover, guide…

Kristin O'Brien, you gifted me with the strength and the language to connect to my warrior archetype during my troubling quarantine times. Training Mace with you as my guide is always an epic adventure. I honor the guide and the warrior in you. Thank you for representing warrior strength in my world.

I am so grateful to have met **Dusty Miner** and **Kimberly Miner,** owners of Peak Performance Cardio Kickboxing Burlington, who opened their minds, hearts, and doors to me. I wrote the section, **Beware of the Dog, in Chapter 2,** to honor your trust, your movement practice, and the beautiful space that you shared with me as I prepared my UFE performance.

I am blessed to feel an extraordinary sense of purpose in my life with the persons who have chosen to work with me as their own personal guide: my clients. A special thank you to **Lani Fellowes, Cheryl Clark, Yasmin Costigan, Kathy Macdonald, Kathryn Ingram, Cindy Blake, Agnes Keenan, Michael Amoroso, Connie Clark, Corenne Taylor, Karen Liptrap, Gillian Niblett, Angie Monetta, Edita Drago,** and **Andrea Mindenhall,** who journeyed with me while I birthed this book between 2019 and 2020. Your strength, your wisdom, your insights, your personal discoveries, and the challenges and growth opportunities you brought for me are intertwined in the pages of this book. You are part of this book. Thank you for your wholehearted belief in me.

I am also humbled and thankful for my clients who joined me in countless adventures between 2010 and 2019, and whose courage inspired me to grow, and whose stories planted the seeds for the creation of this book as well.

I am thankful for the courage of my online group, **Energía en Movimiento,** who helped me grow as an online mind and body teacher during quarantine times. Your presence infused me with energy, creativity, and courage to be the best version of myself, even when I felt that I wanted to give up. You are strong, wise, and courageous, and you have grown so much in such a short period of time. Thank you for your trust in me, and I trust that you will continue to use the knowledge you now have of your body, as a tool to understand the world around you. Thank you **Alejandro Díaz**

Energy in Motion

Mercado, Perla Chávez, Sandra Ferrer, Oralia Chávez, Susana Chávez, Alma Chávez, Lupita Díaz Mercado, Verónica Díaz Mercado, Cecilia Díaz Mercado, Lore Ruíz, Laura Garibay, Ruth Falcón, Olivia Chávez, Olga Romero, Mela Pavan, Norma Calette, Fernanda Echeverría, Ana Ceci Bautista, Ofelia Ortíz, and you who joined me to explore the possibilities that the online world can open up for us, to transform into better versions of ourselves.

A very special thank you to **Matt, Mary, Sunday** and **Silas Carter**, as well as **Peter** and **Celia Sage,** for opening your hearts and homes to me, and for being a loving presence in my world of motion, art, and creation. You have always made me feel at home here in Canada.

A heartfelt thank you to **Michelle P.** for being my consultant for the section *Source and Purpose*, and for your presence in my world.

Trish Taylor holds a special place in my heart, the Universe spoke through her and she placed me in the right place and the right time for me to find what I needed for this book to exist. A warm thank you Trish and **Guillaume McMartin**, for being the catalyst for me to awaken my wisdom.

Thank you to **you who I have yet to meet, and learn that you and I belong in each other's worlds.** I am ecstatic to meet you.

Thank you to **you who whispers in my ear,** and who has been a vehicle to assist me in the integration of this material so that I may share it with the world.

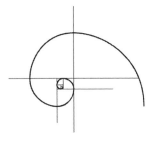

CHAPTER 1
IN THE BEGINNING THERE WAS…

CERTAINTIES

Your eyes are open. Awake, aware, and alive, even though this morning it perhaps took you several seconds to recognize that you were no longer in the dream state. Familiar; the feeling of your body, the sheets on your bed, the lamp on your ceiling, and the certainty of having closed your eyes last night in the same place you are opening them up today. The certainty of waking up day after day, which we often take for granted . . .

A certainty is something solid, like the support of the mattress you sleep on every night, the ground under your feet, or the feeling of this book in your hands. Life is full of certainties, the reassurance that despite all the possible variables, there are certain things we can count on to remain the same; the assurance of unchanging truths that rule this Universe.

The certainty that the sun will rise tomorrow, the law of gravity, the comfort in knowing that you do not need to worry about unexpectedly being expelled from Earth into the oblivion of space, and without a doubt how easily and effortlessly your body regulates temperature and heart rate according to your needs.

This is the thing about certainties; they allow us to consciously forget they exist. And while you do not need to worry about where the moon will be located tomorrow at exactly 2:55 a.m., nor how many eyelashes you should have to protect your eyes, you and I can employ ourselves in other enterprises of our own choosing, as trivial as what Netflix series to watch, or as complex as the decision to go back to school for a master's degree.

What certainties are you currently taking for granted in your life?

I often ask my coaching clients to acknowledge a certainty, any certainty—something as simple as being able to stand on their own feet, or hear the words I am saying—and what difference it would make in their lives if they could no longer count on that. And then I ask them to connect with the meaning and power that such a simple certainty enables in their life. After this quick and simple exercise, I often hear them express how grateful they are for having reconnected with the small yet powerful blessings in their lives.

A certainty is the perfect soil for growth. Careers, houses, and marriages are built on certainties. Certainties make planes fly and investments grow.

In a different category are the certainties that we do not like to be reminded of. Aging is one of them. However exciting it is to a child, it proves disturbing to someone struggling to grasp the changes a human body must experience in order to complete its life cycle. For most, death is a certainty better kept out of sight and out of mind; and yet your beliefs about what happens before you were here, and what will happen afterwards, can powerfully impact the purpose, intensity, and the audacity with which you live your life.

Everything that lives must eventually die. It is a certainty that comes with being alive.

A healthy dose of exploring the urgency of living can enable you to powerfully live the life that you want, and extend that benefit to those you love. It is under the pretense that things remain unchanged that you and I allow ourselves the luxuries of complacency and boredom. It is as if, once in a while, we suffer from time amnesia, which causes us to behave as if we are going to live forever. That is why humans suck at being vampires. Pun intended.

There are small pains to which we might grow accustomed to tolerate in our lives, like hating a job until payday, the several extra pounds on our bodies that have us hiding under a new set of clothes, or the illnesses that come knocking at our doors several times a year. These are just general examples. Every person has their own.

Why is it then that it comes as a shock when such tolerable pains accumulate over time and grow so heavy that a person starts sinking deeper and deeper in the stinky swamp of their stagnant mess?

Thankfully, the Universe has a fail-safe certainty of its own; one that always comes to save the day. Can you guess what that is?

CHANGE

Whereas a *certainty* functions as the foundational soil for growth, it is the passage of time that allows *change* to exert its influence in our bodies, our minds, and our environments. This is necessary for us to experience the lives that we want. If things remained the same, there wouldn't be any space for growth.

But left unchecked, both change and certainties will eventually show you their ugly faces. Certainties evolve into wasting time, and change can be an unpredictable bastard that somehow hardly ever corresponds with our personal agendas.

Change is a certainty in life. Sometimes you see it coming, and sometimes it sneaks up behind you and pulls the carpet out from underneath, leaving you with a sore butt and a sore soul—often too slow for weight loss, the growth in your savings account, and in my case, the process of writing this book. It's always too fast when children grow up, and painfully unexpected when a thriving business turns bankrupt, or brutally definite when someone you love dies.

The darn thing hardly ever seems to be the right dose and at the right time.

Despite knowing of the so-called lottery curse and the troubled lives of the famous, vision boards and daily affirmations are filled with desire for fame and money. History proves, time and again, that it is more likely for an individual to suffer from blessing overload, and self-destruct in the face of massive abundance, than to grow into a better self. Perhaps the story of Adam and Eve, and the demise from paradise, serves as a metaphorical warning of the archetypical code we carry in our genes: the inability to cope with copious amounts of abundance.

Do we really have what it takes to handle a change of such magnitude, like becoming unimaginably rich, when trivial things like the in-laws showing up unexpectedly for dinner, or an unanswered text message, sets us off in a cocktail of stress hormones?

Thankfully, the amount of change you and I are more likely to deal with is pretty manageable. As atrocious as feeling the *shock* from getting fired, the *grief* from the unexpected loss of a loved one, or the *rage* upon encountering a relationship betrayal, we are most certainly capable of building back up a renewed and improved version of ourselves.

When any of my coaching clients verbalize that they are experiencing a period of overwhelming change, I ask them to do an exercise, which I would like to share with you so that you may use it if you are now experiencing an overwhelming situation, or have it for when you need it. The goal of it is to alleviate stress and anxiety, much like relieving pressure from a pressure cooker, and experience a measure of mental clarity that can be used to take focused action, instead of worrying about all that is not within your control.

Grab a piece of paper and, at the top, write the source of overwhelm or change. Divide the page into two columns. Under column one, make note of everything that is outside of your control in this situation. Under column two, write everything that is within your control. Next, fold the paper so that you can no longer see what is in column one. Observe carefully the items on the list of column two, and choose one or two items from your list to take action on right now, or today at the latest.

Inaction is one of the main sources of stress and anxiety in the face of massive change. Several clients have reached out to me immediately after having taken a small measure of action, describing how much lighter and empowered they feel.

While you or any person at any given moment might feel like they are failing at handling change elegantly, it is worth remembering that the same energy that moves a star across the sky is the same energy that creates change in our lives. And if you want to understand that enormous amount of energy a little better, let us have a chat about tomatoes.

TOMATOES

Have you ever wondered, when it comes to change, how it is that the same set of circumstances will have one person raise to their absolute best self, while it will crush another person's spirit?

Unlike growing tomatoes—where you can provide the exact same set of circumstances and have them grow big, red, and juicy—humans, on the contrary, would absolutely fail at being tomatoes. In the same soil and under the same sun, one will metaphorically die while another one thrives. Unfortunately, this is also the case in the literal sense.

Take for example the following case scenario. *Person number one* gets fired unexpectedly after twenty years of working in the same company: no severance package, main source of income for a family of four, no back-up plan or savings. Not without its set of complications, fast forward three years later, and this person has opened his or her own business, triplicating his or her income, and is now enjoying a vacation with his or her whole family on a cruise to Europe.

Person number two gets fired unexpectedly after twenty years, under the exact same set of circumstances. Fast forward three years later, and he or she is broke, divorced, heavily drinking, and unfortunately will not find a reason to continue living.

Words like *work ethic*, *family values*, *resilience*, and *grit* are being thrown like grenades between gaping generations, in an attempt to understand the contrast of both ends of the spectrum. But to oversimplify it to upbringing or labels, would isolate even more those individuals whose saving grace lies in the support of the community. Oversimplifying and labeling, boxes all of us and excludes us from the creative power to move forward in innovative ways. Oversimplifying and labeling puts us all in a position of victimhood, not at cause for change.

At the end of the day, *person number one*, upon his or her return from cruising in paradise, comes back to the society that collectively feels the impact from the demise of *person number two*.

Despite the subconscious sense of interconnectedness we all share but few are aware of, the larger questions still remain. How can some people use tomatoes to make tomato juice and create multimillion-dollar businesses, while other people just helplessly watch the tomatoes rot on the ground?

After 10+ years of experience as a coach and personal guide, helping people experience breakthroughs with their bodies and their minds, I have heard a lot of ways to justify the mystery of why some people thrive and others don't: timing; good luck; education; the people of influence you know; having a passionate personality, an outward personality, an aggressive personality; studying the market; studying the competition; working hard; working smart; putting it in your vision board; stating your daily affirmations; etc., etc., etc.

Even though no one seems to agree on the exact formula, without a doubt every person on this planet has the potential to live a healthy, happy, and a wealthy life. You have that potential too. I know it! In this Universe, it only takes the belief of one person to have something come to fruition, and that person doesn't necessarily have to be you right now. I believe for you, and if you do too, that makes two of us!

Those individuals who have achieved the unimaginable, have the same 24 hours you have. Perhaps it is not just a matter of how they use their time that is different, but also how they use their mind.

But you are you, and you are unique, and this book will take you on a journey to open your mind so that you too can grow into a juicy tomato when the time is right.

> *"Life is the most difficult exam.*
> *Many people fail because they try to copy others,*
> *not realizing that everyone has a different question paper."*
> ~ Unknown

DARKNESS

And so the sun rises again, and with it the certainties of the following day arrive...

Your eyes are open. Awake, aware, and alive, even though this morning it perhaps took you several seconds to recognize that you were no longer in the dream state. Yet today, something feels unfamiliar: the feeling of your body, the sheets on your bed—or is it the light bulb in your ceiling? Maybe it is time to change the color of the walls, you wonder. You can't really tell what it is, yet something just looks or feels different.

You get out of bed, perhaps on the same side you have been getting out on for most of your life. Like a well-oiled machine that no longer needs recalibrating, you then proceed to the execution of your perfectly crafted morning routine. As you brush your teeth, you run through your mind the 10 things you are most thankful for today, in no particular order: number one, your loving spouse and wonderful children; number two, your perfect health; number three, having a job that provides for your family and yourself; number four, having a roof over your head; number five...number ten.

There is usually comfort and pride in listing the certainties you are blessed with, yet these emotions seem to be missing today. You feel it again. Something feels different; something just doesn't feel right.

You check the size of your yoga pants and the number on the scale; you stare at yourself in the mirror, stick out your tongue, and put your hand on your forehead like people do in the movies to check for illness, to try to find the source of this uncomfortable difference, but you cannot put your finger on it.

Is this how it started for Eve, the day she decided to eat the cursed apple that got her and Adam kicked out of paradise? It's not like that apple tree hadn't been there all along.

For some people, change starts deep down in the unconscious, and it slowly makes its way to the surface. The trigger might be an experience that creates a contrast. It could be as simple as hearing a motivational phrase on the radio that makes you feel mildly uncomfortable, to working in an office where everyone is talking about their WOD (workout of the day) and the new keto-friendly recipe they are cooking for tonight's dinner, as you eat the hamburger you picked up on your way to work. Becoming upsettingly uncomfortable, you start wronging yourself for not wanting what they want, and thinking that maybe it's finally time to buy the $12.99 "train-at-home-like-a-pro" program that has been popping on your online feed, despite the fact that you truly hate working out.

For others, change comes in the form of an accident, sickness, a death in the family... an abrupt and undeniable change so permanent and final that there is no turning back.

And while we are busy living and rushing to work, or with the kids who are already fighting in the kitchen waiting for their breakfast, and then busy at work with meetings about more meetings, and then answering emails about scheduling even more meetings, the discomfort takes root.

While we scroll through our social media more times a day than we can count, and extend our working days because "there just isn't enough time in the day" to get it all done, the discomfort grows.

And after our dose of preferred screen time, we lay down in bed at night without being able to fall asleep, left in the darkness to hear the whispers of our undealt-with emotions and limiting decisions, staring at the dark face of our own discomfort.

IN LIGHT OF AWARENESS

Change presented me with challenges that unraveled in the form of wronging myself all the time: wronging myself at home and at work, feeling like no matter how hard I worked, I was never enough; not feeling happy or fit or wealthy enough as I scrolled through social media, feeling envious of my best friend when she decided she was going back to school for a master's; looking in the mirror and hating myself, ultimately becoming the darkness no one wanted to have around in their lives, and feeling like it was unsafe to share my thoughts and emotions.

I suffered alone. My only outlet was my journal. Over the years, I have collected personal stories of all colors, some of which have been inspiration for the material of this book. I would like to share them with you so that you may find comfort in knowing you are not alone. Whenever you go through a rough patch in your life, know that there is always a trail of light for you to find your way. You can access and read my *online journal* at EnergyInMotionBook.com.

Whether change happens gradually and underneath the surface, or it feels as if you have been slapped in the face, the result is an irreversible shift in the axis of your world. Comfort is no longer found in sameness. Your old life starts feeling a bit too tight. Despite all efforts to ignore or resist it, the evidence of it comes back again and again, spiraling into bigger and bigger circles of discomfort. No wonder depression, stress, and anxiety are a hot topic in today's world. Left unattended, this *call to change* sometimes spirals into a self-destruction trajectory.

There is a type of crustacean that outgrows its shell several times in its lifetime. It is at its most vulnerable when it changes shells—any animal could eat it. But in order to grow, it must venture out into the sea in search of a bigger shell. Humans are much like crustaceans: In order to grow, we need to change shells every so often. In the process, it is normal to feel vulnerable, and also an odd mixture of positive and negative emotions as we shed that which no longer serves us. Leaving the safety of the comfortable and certain past, we set out to explore new territory in search of our next perfect shell.

The search is often confusing as we set out with an idea of what we want; sometimes what we want keeps changing along the way. Sometimes we don't know exactly what we want until we find it. All the while, we feel exposed and vulnerable, our tender sides exposed to the real or imaginary predators of the deep dark.

Change is lurking in your unconscious mind and behind the curtains in your bath; it drives to work with you on the backseat, and rests on the headboard of your bed while you sleep. You choose to ignore it, but you can't deny it. Something has changed; something is always changing, and the discomfort that comes along oddly seems to bring back capsules from the past, containing aspects of you that are incomplete.

"Familiar" no longer feels safe. It starts manifesting itself in small corners of your life—triggering you in the voice of your best friend, the image that stares back at you in the mirror, and in the posts from your colleagues on social media, which annoy the hell out of you. It can be swept underneath carpets and flushed down the toilet, but only for a little while.

This era of introspection is both a blessing and a curse. You are no longer doomed to repeat your parents' mistakes, nor to manifest the self-fulfilling prophecies of your upbringing like Freud thought. Yet that means you have to step up to the plate and take ownership for where you put your focus. In this day and age, it is cool to be kind, compassionate, and even spiritual. There is no shortage of coaches, healing modalities, seminars, and books in which to find answers.

Why is it then that so much confusion and turmoil remain within you?

There is a war waging inside of you—opposing forces that call you in different directions: You want to grow, while being unable to let go of the safety and comfort of the familiar past; you want to feel complete, while you obsess over what you don't have; you have a constant desire to feel alive, while choosing to bury emotions you don't like. Contrast scares you. It certainly scared me before I discovered that it serves a specific purpose.

This book does not claim to have solutions to your problems. The mission of *Energy in Motion, How to Unleash Your Mind and Take Action Now*, is to present you with the concepts and processes that will allow for you to self-actualize. To *self-actualize* means to embody in physical form or action that which you have learned and that which you desire.

Take this opportunity to find the perfect answer, while I guide you in a deep dive into the obscure chambers of your mind, some of which you weren't aware existed, or where you have not dared to go alone before.

Open your mind to the idea of breakthroughs, which will happen any time you integrate a piece of the outside world with your world within; and get used to the idea of taking purposeful action to move out from ever again feeling stuck and without options.

Change is a certainty of life, and it is all around us—just look at the time, and notice if the seconds ever stop. Being busy is good when being busy has a purpose. Being busy just to be busy is not good enough anymore. Being busy does not feed your soul and, eventually, it can sum up to the pain of wasting a lifetime.

Walking around with a heavy backpack of unresolved issues, and dealing with emotional flare ups in the face of change, is you being busy putting out fires instead of living your life with purpose and intention. There are those who cannot see that, and they remain stuck for years and years, having the same complaints and the same conversations over and over again, falling victim to the economy, their boss, the weather, their parents, or the spouse they chose!

Placing the blame outside is the easier way out. But where then are the correct answers? Follow your brain or follow your heart? Think logically or go with your gut?

Why does it always have to be an either-or choice? What if you instantly had access to cohesively using the brain, the heart, and the gut, to know what the right answer is for you, in the face of any decision, no matter how big or small?

Most of the material that I have studied is either spiritual or scientific, poetic or literal, scholarly or artistic. In my dissatisfied search for cohesion, I created *Energy in Motion*, with the intention to integrate disciplines in order to make better sense of the machinery we were given to transform our realities. All of the pieces are meant to work as a unit of power.

Despite being of utmost value to humanity, perhaps the lack of humor is one of the reasons religious scriptures lack in popularity. Knowing this, I decided to add a bit of humor to spice up my book. Enlightenment doesn't always have to be so boring.

Change by effect and pain? Or change by cause and choice, having fun while you do it? That is the question, and that is your choice.

Are you ready to play some mind games?

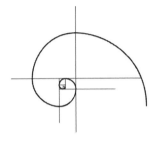

CHAPTER 2
MIND GAMES

HOW TO SHORT-CIRCUIT YOUR BRAIN

Your brain has a fascinating story of its own to tell you. Perhaps in understanding this evolutionary tale, you can begin to understand some of the most shocking exploits of human behavior you can see on a daily basis, both in yourself and others.

The oldest part of the human brain is the brain stem and the cerebellum, also called the *reptilian brain*. A tale contained within the name itself, this ancient brain ruled the first creatures that roamed the Earth: the cold-blooded reptiles. It continues to be a trait we share in common with crocodiles and sharks, 240 million+ years later.

The reptilian brain contains the code to control and regulate the body's vital functions, such as heart rate, body temperature, and adequate breathing rate, among others.

Several thousand years after the oversized reptiles ruled Earth, the first mammalian brains bloomed the *limbic system,* which contains a small portion, approximately the size of an almond, called the *amygdala*. Among other fascinating functions, the amygdala, which is also an important part of the human brain, is also known as *the house of fear.*

The amygdala flares up in light of any situation perceived consciously or subconsciously as an uncertainty or as a threat. And what is more uncertain than change itself? Your amygdala thrives when things stay the same. It may seem the amygdala is not your "amiga," except that its most important role is self-preservation, and it is ruthless when it comes to it. It is thanks to the amygdala that our species survived and evolved into *Homo sapiens*, where the seed of consciousness and self-awareness began to awaken.

One of the most recent parts of the brain, in the history of its evolution, is the *prefrontal cortex*, physically located in the upside and forefront of the brain. Some of its main functions are concerned with the complexity of the human behavior, the unique expression of your personality, self-awareness, empathy, abstract thought, goal setting, and the ability to access future possibilities.

The prefrontal cortex lights up anytime you set a new goal for yourself, in knowledge of the possibility of a raise, and with wide open spaces, among other things of expansive nature, and anything that is perceived as an adventure. Your prefrontal cortex thrives with the imagined possibilities contained in the future, and with the exciting perceptions in the journey ahead. Perhaps this is the part of the brain that drove nomadic life and impossible excursions across the sea to find new lands.

If your brain was a car, the amygdala would be the *brake*, concerned with the permanence of familiar territory and the unchanging past, and the prefrontal cortex would be the equivalent to the *accelerator*, excited about driving head on into the uncharted territory of the future.

What do you think would happen to a car if both the accelerator and the brake were to be pressed at the same time? Maybe you were a precocious, scientifically inclined teenager, and you actually conducted this experiment, but in case you weren't, I would like to satisfy your recently awakened curiosity on this matter. Thankfully, there is a vast record on the internet, of people whose scientific curiosity did get the best of them, and for the purposes of this chapter, I will summarize my findings for you.

Largely dependent on the model of the car, it would spin on its wheels before either the transmission or the radiator, or some other part, burns out, or the car would go on auto lock and not move at all.

If your brain ever feels like it's stuck and unable to make a decision, or spinning out of control or about to short-circuit, it is because you are pressing both the accelerator and the brake at the same time! Both the amygdala and the prefrontal cortex communicate with the rest of your body through a cocktail of hormones, and when both parts get fired up, it feels less like a party and more like a war is being fought within you.

You are not crazy, if the thought ever crossed your mind. If it is of any help, at least you can now name the two warring parts inside your brain, which cause so much disruption and turmoil.

"Are You Feeding the Dog or the Wolf?" is a fascinating multilayered resource I have created for you, to explore if you have been feeding the amygdala or the prefrontal cortex. If you would love to dive deeper into the inner workings of your brain, you can find this on my website, in the *Resources* section.

Did you know that some of the biggest problems in your life can be solved by simply changing a word? Words have power. Some words have the power to trap you, while others have the power to free you. The following mind game will challenge you to look at the labels you are choosing to use, with a critical mind.

BRAIN IS NOT MIND

There is a collective belief that we, the human species, only use about 10% of our brain. Such a statement, if approached critically, should then be followed by the question: *What then is the purpose of the other 90% of it?*

If 90% of the brain is doing nothing, then you and I are cursed to carry around an estimate of three pounds of useless grey matter inside our skulls! No wonder our heads feel very heavy sometimes.

Can you find anything that exists in nature that does not serve a purpose? I can't. I also interviewed 20 of my clients, and they could not come up with anything that upon further investigation wasn't eliminated. I invite you to play this game with me, and if you know of something that exists in nature that does not serve a purpose, connect with me through my website, and we will spark a research conversation.

So, assuming everything in nature serves a purpose, why would our brains be any different? Even though we humans like to behave as though we are above the laws of nature, we abide by them, and it is a simple matter of logic to observe that the other 90% of our brains must indeed serve a purpose.

The unexplored belief that humans can only use 10% of their brain capacity, subconsciously translates into a personal experience that 90% of your brain is inaccessible to you in this lifetime, and therefore you might lack the means to control 90% of what happens in your life. Your subconscious mind might be jumping to all sorts of conclusions without you being aware of it, and that is why it is important to bring them to the light of the aware mind. What you don't know, or in this case the belief you accepted without further investigation, can harm you.

I have found this particular belief to be disempowering to a lot of my clients; that is until I helped them conduct further investigation.

With all the breakthroughs that human kind has experienced, from medicine to astrophysics, how is it that we have erred when it comes to making the best use of our own motherboard, the brain?

Truth is, we haven't; we are simply experiencing a collective semantic error.

For the most part, language helps you define and understand the world that surrounds you, but when the word you have chosen limits you in any way, you are cursed to suffer inside a prison of your own doing. A *limiting belief* is either a word, a choice, a belief, or a decision you have consciously or subconsciously made about yourself or the world around you, that is limiting and therefore disempowering.

I often help my seminar attendees to eradicate a collective limiting belief by reframing the situation. Like the word implies, *reframing* means to put a word in another context or look at it under another light. I can often hear wonderful exclamations after using this technique, and although I won't be able to hear yours, say a loud "WOW!" if you like what you are about to learn.

If you were to consider that we have misused the word *brain* for the organ, in an attempt to describe the presence of *mind*—the place within us perceived to house our consciousness—and by applying the logic that everything in nature serves a purpose, that would mean that your brain is working just as creation intended it to. In observing that, it is more a matter of understanding the depths of the human mind and human consciousness that confuses us. We can now move on to considering a new set of questions.

Philosophy, theology, psychology, sociology, quantum theory, neuro-linguistic programming, and neuroscience are but a few disciplines that for several hundred years have constantly been pushing the boundaries of how we perceive and define consciousness.

Energy in Motion

Even though we are as far from grasping the complexities of the human mind as we are from exploring the depths of the Universe, these various disciplines seem to agree on one item in particular. From the scientific communities, to the most spiritual yogis of the world, there is an understanding that about 90% of what runs the show in our lives is happening in the background of our awareness, on an unconscious level, and only 10% happens at the conscious level of our awareness. So, yes, the percentages were accurate but in a different context.

This might be an oversimplified yet interesting way to observe how in attempting to use 10% of our mind to navigate changes and problems in our lives, the results are often frustration, emotional distress, disease, anger, pain, regret, procrastination, waste of talent and time, and so many other forms of existential crises.

What if I told you that you are used to muscling your way through life with only 10% of your mind? Don't get me wrong; a lot of amazing things can be achieved with it, but the downfall is that it takes longer, and sometimes the conscious mind falls trap to its own limitations. What if I told you that 90% of your mind has been trying to communicate with you for most of your adult life, to help you move 10 times faster in the direction you want to go, but you simply haven't been able to decode the message? How would your life change if all of a sudden you had nine times more the mind power to do anything you want?

Would you like to know, first of all, if that is possible?

No one has yet found a boundary for the potential housed within our minds; in fact, up to date, it is considered unlimited. So, in theory, the answer is yes, but this leaves you feeling the same way you felt before we substituted the word *brain* for *mind*, without a clear answer. On top of that, trying to map or navigate the concept of *unlimited* is like trying to put infinity inside a Tupperware container so that you can have it for lunch later. "Unlimited" is a pretty intimidating concept, to say the least.

Your unconscious mind has a built-in fail-safe to prevent you from triggering the war between the amygdala and the prefrontal cortex, by allowing you to absorb information in a linear way, much in the same way you are reading this book: one line at a time.

By simply continuing on to the next section, and learning more about your unconscious mind, you are laying the foundations that will allow you to open up the communication channels with it, and enable you to understand what it has been trying to tell you all this time.

All you need to do right now is to continue ahead with the journey of discovery, one line at a time.

BROKEN MINDS

When it comes to the human species, there are several qualities that unequivocally set us apart from other sentient beings. They are, to say the least, both a blessing and a curse.

Have you ever seen a lion hesitating on a kill, wondering if he should hunt a zebra instead of a buffalo on any particular day? The assumption is that they hunt and kill on pure instinct, and hesitate on that instinct as well. On the other hand, I have found myself prey to the cognitive ability that I have to count calories, when struggling with the decision to eat a donut if it doesn't fit my macros. I hesitate because I can, not because I need to.

But the ability that you and I have to use the functions of the higher brain, more often than not, seem to spark inner conflict worthy of a political debate. It's hard to experience peace and quiet when all the unanswered questions and incomplete aspects of ourselves start arguing with each other.

Was there ever a time where we could fall sleep without lamenting the "what ifs" and the "should haves?" Was there ever a time when life was simpler?

Yes.

Somewhere between the ages of two and seven, the boundaries between what is real and what is not, had not been established. It was one of the most magical times in our lives, where playing with imaginary friends from the future, flying down the house corridors, and growing up to be an astronaut was as real as cereal.

When I was about six years old, my grandfather used to tell me that if I ate too much salt, I would grow hair on the back of my hands, and my fingers would shrivel and turn into goat hooves. Although having hooves for hands didn't sound too bad to me, I worried that I wouldn't be able to draw cool pictures anymore, and so I stopped eating salt altogether.

Despite the fact that you and I know, as adults, that it is not possible to grow hooves by eating too much salt, and maybe you would rather work from home than be an astronaut, the world seemed a little happier when presents magically appeared under our trees, less lonely when our imaginary friends visited, and more full of potential when dragons dominated the skies.

As children grow in awareness of the limitations tied to being a child, they start to develop an intense desire to grow up so that they can be allowed to play with the grownups and do all the cool things that grownups do, like driving a car, going to work, and buying things with money—things most adults would label as overrated. You get the paradox.

And so whether it is because children actually want to grow up, or because they are told to do so, their minds start taking detailed notes on what adults accept as reality versus what they don't. Somewhere around the age of seven, the *critical faculty* gets created. The critical faculty is the part of us that cares to distinguish what is real and what is not, according to the collective agreements we have as humanity. The deep-rooted sense of belonging is as strong in an adult as it is in a child, and this part, generally speaking, cares about fitting in with the human race.

When the critical faculty is created, it is initially a thin veil that filters the world into what is real, sequential, and logical, and belongs in the conscious mind, separating it from what is ethereal, fantastical, and imaginary, and part of the uncharted realm of the unconscious mind. Generally speaking, with age, the critical faculty tends to thicken the more a child, a teenager, and a young adult continues to succeed at passing the tests of what it means to be a functioning adult.

In the adult mind, the thickness of this boundary varies from person to person. For example, an individual hardened by life, or someone whose job depends on having a thick critical faculty, like a police officer or an immigration officer, will likely rely on having a thick critical faculty to properly execute their role. On the other hand, visionaries like Steven Spielberg and George Lucas, everyday gamers, and even people who believe everything the tabloids say about aliens, typically have a thin critical faculty.

The adult minds that appear to function without a critical faculty are labeled in the extremes as either faulty or genius. The chosen labels unequivocally set these individuals apart from what is perceived as the "normal" functioning adult, for better and for worse. It is speculated that Albert Einstein and Steve Jobs, two of the most impactful minds, fell somewhere on what is called the autistic spectrum.

Speculation and labels aside, individuals with minds like these show us the lesson that in order to transcend what is real and possible, one must travel to the world of the invisible, and much like a child, use abilities such as imagination and creativity to grab that which doesn't exist and bring it back to the world of reality.

In a world that idolizes science and logic, you will be surprised to learn the advice that Albert Einstein has for the upbringing of brilliant children:

"If you want your children to be intelligent, read them fairy tales. If you want your children to be more intelligent, read them more fairy tales."

To the adult mind, this is a message to let go of the need to continuously define what is real and what is not, and to let go of the leash on what we think is possible. This is a message to dare to travel to the invisible world, and to bring back a new way of thinking and being that will transcend the problems that are keeping individuals and societies stuck.

Access a quick reference map of the parts of the mind, in the *Resources* section on my website. And now let's take a deeper dive; let me introduce you to the part of you that is fully equipped to travel to the invisible world, and bring back some of the answers to get you from stuck to moving.

THE UNCONSCIOUS MIND

Perhaps you are most familiar with the word *unconscious* as a state of being in which you are neither aware nor awake, and therefore have no control over. As I have previously discussed, along with the concept of *change*, it seems that the human species, generally speaking, has a big problem with not having a handle on things. The concept of *not having control over* a portion of our minds, doesn't often sit too well either, even though our *conscious* state is already quite troublesome to say the least.

Have you ever turned off the lights, and while your eyes adjust, find yourself staring into a pitch-black room where the darkness seems unending, and noticed how uncomfortable that makes you feel?

As a child, my attempt at reaching the kitchen for a midnight snack, without turning the lights on, was often cut short by the panic that ensnared me after staring into the empty black corridor ahead of me.

Looking into the shallow depths of unending darkness is an overwhelming experience that brings both awe and fear. Being in the presence of an abyss, a hole, a cave, the night sky—any blackness blacker than black—can trigger a primal fear in the pit of your stomach, and chills down your spine. Despite the fact that you now know that this is an amygdala-driven behavior, and a natural part of your survival mechanisms, it still leaves you wondering why imagined monsters have so much power over you.

The answer lies in the unconscious mind. Children under the age of seven are most familiar with this domain, as they swim in it often, and they will swear to you that monsters are very real.

Energy in Motion

The oversimplified diagram of the iceberg is perhaps the most ingenious way to illustrate the complex relationship between the conscious and the unconscious mind. You might have come across it yourself in psyche class or when looking up Freud on the internet. There are records throughout history and throughout ancient cultures all over the world, which indicate a sense of *knowing* of a part of our psyche that is hidden from our conscious, waking life. Our modern world is privileged to have a choice of practices that range from a classroom to a one-on-one practice, from recreational to therapeutic, from physical to conceptual, with the goal to assist any individual that chooses to journey into the deep chambers of the mind.

The unconscious mind is the part of the mind connected to the world of the invisible. On one hand, it speaks the language of imagination, fantasy, emotions, hopes, and dreams, and on the other hand, it is in charge of the self-regulating functions of your body that keep you alive, all of which happens in the background of your awareness.

When you get hurt or sick, how does your body know to return to its natural healthy state? It happens as if by magic, and it is because the perfect blueprint for your body is stored within your unconscious mind.

When your conscious mind falls asleep at night, you naturally enter the realm of the unconscious mind through your dreams, where time, space, and matter can be bent at will and follows no logical rules.

To your conscious mind, where logic lives, the unconscious mind is unfamiliar and unsettling territory, because it does not follow the rules of what we call reality, and tolerates a relationship as long as the boundary of what is real and what is not is quite clear.

The unconscious mind is like a genie from a magic lamp, with unending capabilities and wishes, where one of its favorite phrases is, "Your wish is my command"; whereas the conscious mind likes the certainty of, "I'll believe it when I see it."

It has been my personal experience, during initial conversations with clients, that subjects that reside in future possibilities trigger an unsettling response. Fascinating as it is, future possibilities can be a concept so abstract that they are possibly perceived by the conscious mind as preposterous as *infinity, unending darkness,* and making up with the unconscious mind. The term "unconscious mind" elicits a similar response in coaching circles, to the point that some choose to soften it up by calling it "subconscious mind" instead—a matter of semantical preference, but worth exploring the reason behind it.

Your unconscious mind is simply a set of dark rooms in your psyche for you to explore and discover. You can call it *unconscious*, *subconscious*, or *hello darkness my old friend* if you'd like. The journey to the world of the invisible and the infinite initially feels a lot like the black corridor that stops a child from getting the midnight snack, but in allowing the eyes of your conscious mind to adjust to the darkness, and getting past the fear, you can start to make out the shape of the objects within, and play with other senses like intuition and creativity. This might as well be the answer you seek to expand in consciousness and travel to the realm where the answers to your problems are created.

Despite the collective agreements we have about what reality is and how consciousness works, at its core, it is still a personal experience. Much like religion and politics, heated debates often arise in an attempt to grasp these concepts; and perhaps in the end, it will always be a matter of personal speculation.

The material you are reading will continue to inspire your own set of personal questions. Questions are mind quests that ache to be answered, and they represent an organic and natural modality of mind growth. The need to ask them arises when the concepts that fascinate you meet with the contexts that I present to you through this book, at a moment of utmost importance.

The question in your mind will burn the most when it is first formulated; and if unanswered, its importance will slowly fade away. It is precisely due to this that I will encourage you to keep a journal next to you while you read Energy in Motion, so that you may write all of your questions down.

I am curious to know how many of the questions you come up with can be answered within the pages of this book, or if you and I will connect, and a second book will be created out of your unanswered questions. The possibilities are endless, much like the quests you and I can choose to take on, and a lot like any journey into the world of the invisible.

In the meantime, the final section of "Mind Games" contains an important warning that you must read before you continue the journey ahead…

BEWARE OF THE DOG

"Check your Ego at the door," reads the sign at the entrance of the kickboxing facility, around the corner from my house. "Ego" is written with a capital E, as if to subtly remind me to be aware that it might put up a BIG fight.

Just like my favorite kickboxing facility, there are certain places one cannot enter without a ritual of sorts, a metaphorical *shedding of skins.* Showing up to work without leaving your home problems at home, taking a class thinking you know more than the teacher, or entering a place of worship without respect for the dress code, are great examples of inappropriate social appearances of the ego.

Another great example is the sign you will often encounter at the entrance of yoga studios and other training facilities during winter time: "No outdoor shoes beyond this point." If removing your ego at the door were as easy as removing all your winter gear, I would like to think that most people in their right minds would choose to do so.

But the problem with the ego is that it is a sneaky construct that lives in our minds, which hides or distorts aspects of our personalities. Metaphorically speaking, it would behave in such a way that even though your intention was to follow instructions, you would find yourself standing in the middle of the padded mats, with a trail of destructive salt and goo behind you, wondering what the hell just happened—not only being in an awkward and uncomfortable position yourself, but also impacting the other students while everyone waits for the facility owners to clean up the mess so that the class can start.

If you have ever had to own up to a mistake, which you weren't aware you were making until someone had enough courage to show you how you were being in the eyes of others, you know exactly what I am talking about.

We don't err intentionally, but when the ego works underneath the surface of the conscious mind, there are aspects of ourselves that we can only become aware of when having a reality check through a mindful and courageous soul that shows us how we have erred.

Energy in Motion

This chapter of my book functions as a sort of gateway, and the sign at the top reads "Beware of the Dog."

Depending on how far you have stumbled down the rabbit hole of introspection, you might find that the material I present to you challenges aspects of your conscious mind, your ego, or your definition of reality. Be warned, you cannot enter with the mindset of "you cannot teach an old dog new tricks," because the sign "beware of the dog" is actually talking about yourself. You are the only one who can talk yourself out of learning something new. The dog you should be mindful of is your own "Ego," purposefully written with a capital E, for you to be aware that it often does put up a BIG fight.

To leave you with this warning, without telling you what to do about it, would be like giving you Gizmo, the gremlin, without telling you to never let it get close to water or feed it after midnight. If you missed the awesome 80s, you might want to look up the movie, *The Gremlins*, for reference on this metaphor.

So within the next chapter, you will find five fascinating strategies that I teach my coaching clients as a prerequisite for successfully completing their coaching programs, and for manifesting powerful breakthroughs in their own lives. Not only will these five strategies function as self-assessment tools as you read *Energy in Motion*, but they will also gift you with tools in any area of your life where you are seeking personal growth, such as relationships, business, fitness, financial goals, etc.

Enjoy, and use them often.

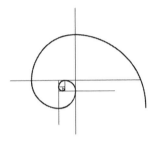

CHAPTER 3
SECRETS OF SUCCESSFUL SHAPESHIFTERS

SHAPESHIFTING FOR BEGINNERS

Shape-shifter, noun
: one that seems able to change form or identity at will.
~ Merriam-Webster Dictionary

Let's say you are reading this book while sitting on a couch after a long day at work, thinking about making yourself a cup of coffee because you can barely keep your eyelids open, and just can't remember this damn paragraph you have already read three times.

You don't even manage to summon the strength to get up when your spouse arrives home from work. He/she walks straight to you, but somehow something is off. He/she then cracks open about the news of having received an offer to join the firefighting force, after five years of strenuous applications that you both have endured.

You get up from the couch as though a firecracker exploded underneath you, pun intended, and you cry and jump and hug them so hard you end up getting an arm pump, like when you do bicep curls at the gym. What happened to the heaviness and tiredness you had felt just moments before the arrival of such fabulous news? It was there, and then it wasn't. In fact, you are then so infused with energy that you stay up all night celebrating with your spouse.

This is an example of shapeshifting states based on an external event. Changing states based on an external event is often a reaction, and a reaction is an energy form that perpetuates the source that created the state. It is great when it is a good state like joy or excitement, but not so great when it is something like anger or sadness.

States are decisions you make about yourself and how you want to feel in regard to an external event experienced in the past, present, or future. They usually happen within fractions of a second at the subconscious level.

They are habitual in nature. One example would be if you habitually get moved to a state of tenderness in the presence of a baby, or if the sight of a baby in person or in a Facebook post makes you experience feelings of tenderness, whether you are sitting on the toilet or on a bench by the lake. And because they are habitual, they can also be as challenging to reprogram as an adult trying to drop the habit of eating cereal at night, only to find that four months later, that person is still trying to drop the habit.

Changing states is often a challenge to those who haven't become aware that a state can be commanded or created from inside, and used to create a ripple effect that extends to others. Changing a state at will is being at cause. Changing states at will is the power to create and define the reality you are about to experience rather than being defined by it.

Reality is constantly being created by your interaction with others, who as far as I know are a Universe of their own, and who sometimes do not share the same views and values you have. Perhaps you are not fully in control of your environment and everything that happens to you, but you can either let the exterior dictate your interior how to feel, or you can access that part of you that no one else can, and create a state of your own choosing.

The first step to learning how to shapeshift is to acknowledge that there is space somewhere inside of you that absolutely no one other than you can ever access. For some people, that space is found within their minds; and for others, within their hearts. Do you know where to find that space within you?

You can start practicing shapeshifting in the comfort of your own house, with a technique called *State Elicitation*. First name a feeling, emotion, or state of being that you would like to experience. Then close your eyes and remember a specific time in the past when you felt that way. What were you doing, seeing, hearing, smelling, etc.? Let your imagination play so strongly that you start sensing the memory spread through your body, and let yourself really feel it.

When you are ready, open your eyes and ask yourself the following set of questions: If I was in that state of (name the feeling, emotion, or state you wish to elicit), how would I stand and how would I sound? What would I say? How would I react to (name a situation that is relevant)? What questions would I ask, and to whom? What information would I seek? How would I act and speak right now? What would I do in the next five minutes, hour, day, or week? And then take one action item.

Action is the spark of life and the fuel that feeds the emotion of your choosing. Action is the final stage to embody energy in motion. Action will move you forward in creating an immediate future based on the state that you desire to perpetuate. The missing piece in the movie *The Secret,* which slowed the creative possibilities of many, was the understanding that action is the fuel of change, and whether big or small, beyond creating a vision board, continuous action is needed to perpetuate the energy of that which has been created in the invisible world of the mind.

The practice of this technique at home is useful because once you are out your door, the world will give you plenty of opportunities to test your shapeshifting abilities—anything from finding your neighbor's dog's poop in your yard, to receiving any sort of devastating news. Do you want to be a storm of reactive emotion perpetuating the negative energies around you, or do you want to have a clear mind to take purposeful action and redirect the course of the next few moments and possibly the rest of your life?

Useful states to consider while reading this book: awe, humor, childlike wonder, scientific curiosity, creative curiosity, and of course, an open mind.

GROWTH IN THREES

A tree grows the only way a tree knows how to: upwards, downwards, and sideways. It grows from the moment the seed is nurtured by the ground, and until the day that it dies. It grows and grows, for it knows nothing else than how to grow and be a tree.

A person, on the other hand, is both blessed and cursed with having a sentient consciousness and free will. A person can choose to behave like a tree, or dress up and attend cosplay events, or lay on the couch for days on end.

Ready, willing, and able: These are three states necessary for personal growth. Ready can mean that it is the perfect time to grow; willing, that you are choosing to say yes to an opportunity because it resonates with you; and able, that you have the financial, personal, and/or material means to go ahead with the adventure.

Someone who is ready and willing but not able, might not have the resources necessary to pay or get to a seminar happening across the country.

Someone who is ready and able but unwilling, perhaps has the means but disagrees with the material being presented.

Someone who is willing and able but not ready, maybe has to

be at home caregiving for a parent, and is not able to take the time to attend a seminar.

When presented with an opportunity to grow or learn in any area of your life, you can check for the presence of the three states described above. If one were to be missing, and you would still like to move forward in growth, simply see what arrangements you can do from your end to move forward with the venture, perhaps at a later time, with a different instructor, or the time it would take for you to gather the resources you need. You are most powerful when you are self-aware.

COACHABILITY AND TEACHABILITY CUPS

Coachability is a state in which you are accepting of the concepts that a coach, teacher, or book is presenting to you. There are some that you will easily and effortlessly resonate with, and there are others that will test your boundaries. If you find yourself feeling uncomfortable or disagreeing with a piece of information, those are two signs that tell you that your boundaries are being tested.

Personal boundaries are meant to be tested for strength but also for opportunities to expand and change. An unchanging personal boundary in the face of time, might result in a stiff mind and a closed point of view. I am sure you do not think and behave as your parents did, even though they taught you their faith and values. You outgrew some outdated concepts and moved on to seek some of your own.

Teachability is a state in which you are ready and open to learning, much like a fresh sponge that is ready to absorb any liquid that might come in contact with it, or like an empty cup waiting to be filled with fresh, new liquid.

As where *coachability* is your willingness to grow and accept change, your *teachability* index is your capacity and ability to absorb knowledge. Both are requirements for growth. At any given moment, both coachability and teachability can be assessed on a scale from 1–10. This is called a coachability and teachability index.

If you recall a moment studying for any kind of exam, where you wanted to continue studying, but no matter how much effort you put in, or how many times you read and recited the information out loud, you just couldn't remember it. Your head felt swollen and foggy. This is an example of how your coachability index might have been at 10/10, but your teachability index, your capacity to absorb more, was maxed out, leaving you at a 0/10.

A good example of a high teachability index but low coachability index is when during a fitness consultation, a person asks me what the best exercise is to reduce belly fat, to which I kindly reply that their energy would be best spent making nutrition and activity changes for the healthiest and fastest belly fat reduction results, which is probably the same thing they have heard from a dietician, naturopath, doctor, etc. The person often answers, "I know," and proceeds to ask me the same question. I realize then that I am in the face of a low coachability index, and I change my approach so that I can help the person as best as I can.

Teachability and coachability can be imagined as two cups. In an empty state, they are at their most receptive state, and at any given moment, their capacity for receptiveness will fluctuate, and it's supposed to. Upon assessing where you are with both of them, you might decide to take a break from unsuccessfully trying to absorb new information (teachability), or evaluate if the source of information is the appropriate one for you, or if you are simply being stubborn and unwilling to look at things in a new light (coachability).

BEING AT CAUSE

Being at cause means taking ownership for the inner state you are choosing to be in, for how long, and for the action or inaction that follows. It is a real superpower to be proud of.

You might not see how you are in control of the traffic that had you arriving late for a job interview, or the market crash, or the car that hit you from behind, and you do not need to take ownership of any of that in order for you to be at cause *right now*.

Being at cause is an empowered and creative mindset that allows you to focus on solutions and actions, instead of faults and problems. How often do you hear people around you complain about the weather, or the people they work with, or how busy they are, when you know of someone else who would give anything to be in their spot?

Whether life is going great or not, there is someone out there complaining about it.

As children, some might have figured that if they played clumsy, they could skip sports camp and stay home instead to play computer games all summer. Some others might not have had to study as hard as their brothers and sisters, by dumbing themselves down, and getting to play their favorite sport instead. As an adult, the payoff for not being at cause is perhaps not having to make tough decisions or take action, especially when these decisions have major consequences. They would much rather check out, hoping time will pass and situations might get resolved, or someone else might step up instead.

Paradoxically, this erroneous way of "being" could eventually ensnare a person in a subconscious loophole of hell, called *victimhood* or *being at effect*.

If you would not intentionally lock yourself in a small dark space with no water and no food, where it is hard to breathe and you cannot see anything, then why do this mentally? Metaphorically speaking, this is what an unwarranted victim mentality is like—being locked away and cut off from personal power to breathe, move, nurture, and be in control of your life. This suffocating and paralyzing mindset is most often than not a construct of our ego, which wants us to feel so unique that it ends up feeling more like we are alone in this world, because no one could possibly understand what we are going through. The more time someone spends in victim mode, the more stuck in the loophole the person becomes, and the deeper they sink into the hole.

Being at cause is the awareness to acknowledge when this is happening, and having the personal power to step outside this paralyzing state. Being at cause is a choice that happens in the "now," and because every moment is a new "now," it might take many workouts to grow your causation muscle.

To be at cause in any given situation, you can begin by putting your attention on those things inside and outside of yourself that are within your control, and take it away from those you can't control. Review the exercise provided in Chapter 1, *Change*, if you have a specific situation you are dealing with.

Look to see if there is at least one action that you can take right now to be at cause in any situation that has had you feeling stuck; or if unable to do this, ask for help. That in and of itself is an action. Remember, your ego wants you to feel alone and special, but guess what? You are special but never alone.

YES I DO…

… and they lived happily ever after. Or did they?

Just as these three words, spoken at the altar, allow two people to willingly be wed for what they hope will be a lifetime of joy, change must be accepted into our lives, or else it will be a hell of a marriage for a little while.

Change starts with the conscious awareness of the imminent truth that something can no longer remain the same. In this initial stage, it is pretty obvious who is embracing it and who is resisting it, like a kid who doesn't want to shower. Embracing it will likely bring a state of ease and flow, and fighting it will just tire you out until you can fight it no more.

Next, comes the acceptance of what is to come; again, you can walk into it with a smile, with your head held high and with pride in your strengths and abilities, or you can feel uncertain and fearful. Know that both approaches are very human and, as such, there is no right or wrong in either one. Humans are meant to be humans, not gods or superheroes. Vulnerability is an endearing trait of humankind that allows us to develop empathy and compassion for each other.

Finally, engaging with change is a lot like dancing the Tango. It is a beautifully passionate and passive-aggressive dance of forces, with ups and downs and sharp and unexpected turns. It is an opportunity to observe what emotions bubble up, and the opportunity to do something with them; perhaps forgive someone or forgive ourselves, or maybe make a beautiful piece of art, or finally sign up for Tango lessons. Emotions are the energy of life, and we need not be afraid to put ourselves in situations that call them up to rise from death.

Energy in Motion

To say, "Yes, I accept change," is to say yes to living a purposeful and powerful human life, to be ready, willing, and able to make the best of the time and gifts we have been given.

Live on and dance away.

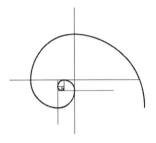

CHAPTER 4
THE FABRIC OF REALITY

SELF-FULFILLING PROPHECIES

For the most part, history is obscured by speculation, and the reality of it defined by those who wrote it. This preamble is an invitation for you to keep that in mind as you read the following chapter.

As told by some, it is said that when the ships of Christopher Columbus first appeared on the horizon of American lands, in 1492, the natives were shocked to see "oddly shaped clouds," and that it wasn't within their capabilities to see the massive ships approaching. They certainly did not have a word to name what they were seeing. A ship that big was something that had never before existed in their world.

Before the arrival of the ships in America, the most prominent Mesoamerican cultures worshiped the god, Quetzalcóatl, the feathered serpent. The worship of this god extended throughout the region, today known as the country of Mexico. Prophets across the land foresaw that one day Quetzalcóatl would return in the flesh to his people.

Quetzalcóatl was believed to be of Caucasian decent, blond with blue eyes, according to some records, which could be explained by speculating that perhaps a lonely Viking got lost, and ended up in Mesoamerican territory and became a worshiped god centuries before the arrival of the Spaniards. This sounds farfetched yet not impossible.

Records also hold that high priests from several regions, along with the prophetic return of the beloved god of wind and knowledge, also predicted the arrival of a different race and the fall of the empires across the land. These were the priests and prophets that delivered the will of the gods to emperors and commoners alike,

Energy in Motion

who knew about the stars and the crops and the ways of the elders. They were pillars of the belief system of Mesoamerica. And so, their word was the law of the gods and the law of reality.

There is a speculative claim that despite massive losses to chicken pox and Spaniard weaponry, had it not been for the prophecy stating that Quetzalcóatl would return, or that the empire would fall, the Aztec empire could have eradicated the threat of the invaders led by Hernán Cortés and other historical Spaniards.

I am not an expert on warfare, but a war cannot be won when doubt and fear have taken a warrior's heart before the enemy has. For the Aztec warriors, the seed of doubt and fear had already been planted by their own spiritual guides. This might very well have been a case of a self-fulfilling prophecy.

What I propose to you then is to observe the idea that the reality you perceive is built upon a frame of reference that takes root in your own past. Whether that frame of reference was obtained conceptually through the narrative or teachings of others, or obtained in an abstract manner by personal experience, such precedent can positively or negatively impact the absorption of incoming new reality. Not only that, just like the natives of America did not have a word to name "ships," because your perception of current reality is connected to your past frame of reference, your intake of it is relatively limited to that which "makes sense" to you and what you currently can name. Any foreign object or concept might be overlooked or perceived as a danger to your current model of the world.

Information is getting subconsciously installed in our brains all the time, through the news, conversations at the office, books we read, and YouTube videos we watch. Because the frame of reference functions in the subconscious mind, much like software installed in computers, it is important to be mindful of our choice to absorb information, and of the sources we choose to absorb it from.

Be mindful of the prophets you choose.

IF YOU HATE A CAT

Anyone that hates cats can only hate them for two reasons. One, they had a bad personal experience with a cat in the past, or two, they became associated with a story someone else told them about a bad experience with a cat.

If you did not know what a cat was, and you were to encounter a cat for the first time in your life, you might laugh at having encountered a tiny lion, proving the point that you would absorb the experience of "cat" based on your understanding of "lion." However if you had never learned of the existence of the feline family in this world, and you encountered a cat, you might pride yourself in having found a new species, or in thinking you were being visited by an alien creature.

The Matrix is the story of Neo, a man who "wakes up" to find he is connected to a super computer inside a pod, where he is being fed the experience of *reality* while being harvested for the use of sentient computers. This movie created a collective frame of reference for the human race to question how we perceive reality, among other fascinating mysteries of the mind.

Fast forward 20 years after *The Matrix* was launched at theatres, and we are now surrounded by documentaries, books, and data, blowing out the epistemological boundaries of what we labelled as impossible 20 years ago. Not only are the long standing records by mythological athletes like Michael Phelps being broken weekly, there is rumor on the internet about a human head transplant having been performed already! And whether this is just internet gossip or not, I know for a fact that a lamb was grown in an artificial uterus. Isn't this the freaky stuff from movies, happening right now in our own lifetimes?

The boundaries of what we as a human race took for possible are being shaken; just look at the advancements within the past 300 years compared to the timeline of humanity. We are living in a key moment in time; a moment of incredible power and possibility. It is of utmost importance that you exist right here and now. But in order to see this, you have to wake up from certain programs of the past that have been running your life without you knowing it, ways of thinking that are outdated, and frames of reference that are leashing your power back.

What you don't know can indeed harm you.

HOW TO SLEEP BETTER AT NIGHT

What you experience as *reality* is very different than what I experience as *reality*. This can help you understand why people cannot agree on such important matters as religious or spiritual beliefs, if being vegan is the answer to heal your body, or the discrepancies in the argument you just had with your spouse. You might already have disagreed with some of the concepts I have presented to you in this book.

Understanding why this happens might possibly help you sleep better at night, and also to have a more amicable relationship with everyone around you.

Any relationship starts by finding common ground, and that common ground is called planet Earth. By being plugged into this rock, along with the other estimated 7.4 billion humans, we share what is called *universal agreements*. This ranges from how we define reality, to a sort of *code of ethics* for being human. The subdivision of continents into countries, treating your fellow human like you want to be treated, the laws of gravitation, and the 24 hours we have in a day are examples of these collective agreements. There are always exemptions to the rule, in the form of some minds that whether by design or choice, do not abide by the same standards.

If you start chunking down into subdivisions within Earth, you will find yourself traveling from the planet to your continent, to your country, to your state or region, to your community, neighborhood, home, and family, until you find you! You are a part of a greater whole, and while you have two eyes, one nose, and a heart and a brain like most humans on this planet, you are still a*bsolutely unique, special, and absolutely irreplaceable and necessary.*

There is absolutely no possible way that there is anyone on this planet, or even in this galaxy or within the infinity of the Universe, who has had the exact same experiences, feelings, cells, neurons, thoughts, and everything else that makes you, *you.* Your "youniquness" is what is reading this book and these words. You and all of your history, language, past, and emotions, and even what you carry over from some of your ancestors, composes layers and layers and layers of the complex uniqueness of you that constructs your reality and your frame of reference to absorb and process it.

Doesn't it make sense then that when someone uses the word "pink elephant" in a conversation in the office's lunchroom, one person laughs and someone else leaves the room enraged? Due to the complex uniqueness of each individual, the same word will trigger a unique and unpredictable response in each one of us. The same word might even trigger a different response in a person, depending on whether its Monday or Friday!

At the age of 16, I visited Spain with my family for the first time. In both Spain and Mexico, my native country, Spanish is the official language. One night at the dinner table, my aunt asked our host to pass her the bottle of "pills" that were next to him so that she could take her medicine with dinner. Little did we know that the word "pill," in Spain, is used to name the female sexual organs. It wasn't until the red faces erupted in laughter that we learned better than to use that word at the dinner table.

If reality is as awkward as puberty, then we might as well take it in with a bit of humor.

LET'S AGREE TO DISAGREE

Think of a person you recently had an argument with, and with whom you still feel incomplete. Ask yourself the following question: "Is it more important to be right or to be happy?"

Hang on to your answer while I help you explore how our minds construct reality. You can obtain a visual diagram on my website to have a better understanding of the concepts presented in the following chapter.

Imagine that a small square has been drawn on a blank piece of paper. That square represents a window, and to you, the observer, reality means whatever you can perceive through such window. This is "what you know you know," because you have intellectually experienced it and experientially lived it. Before you ever drove a car, you knew people around you that did so, and you observed others do it. You studied and passed your written exam, then went on to pass your driver's test, and now you drive a car. This would be a perfect example of an *actualized experience*.

Now, for a moment, consider the empty space on the sheet of paper outside the square. This would be a representation of what you are intellectually aware of but haven't personally experienced. It is a reality within your reach. For example, if you were interested in driving a motorcycle now, you could simply sign up for the upcoming course at a college nearby, and within six months be driving a motorcycle.

Now observe, with your imagination, the space around you wherever you are, and consider this space in relation to your imagined piece of paper of which you are aware but don't know much about. For example, you are aware that some people have developed the skills to fly airplanes, and you might even personally know a pilot. Flying planes is humanly possible; however, you have no idea how you could do that, and perhaps don't even care about doing it.

And then there is all the space outside of your line of sight. You don't know what is going on in Italy at the moment, or on Saturn; and beyond that, an enormous infinity of space and possibility stretches beyond human comprehension. As a child, I used to tell my parents that if the Universe was indeed infinite, then you could always find a yes and a no answer, a truth or falsehood, to anything a person could wonder—a possible or impossible to everything, somewhere out there in the galaxy. You don't know what you don't know. And anything you don't know of will have no prior frame of reference to assist you in understanding what it is.

Energy in Motion

After chunking up to infinity, let's chunk back down to the small square drawn on the page. If you look at the *Constructed Reality* diagram, you will notice that the five senses have been written around the frame: sight, sound, smell, taste and touch. These are the five feedback channels through which we experience, decode, and record reality. The five senses are a perfect example of another *universal agreement,* as these senses are experienced by most humans. The ++ signs in the diagram stand for the possibility that some people experience out of the ordinary perception, as described by a small percentage of the population. Some examples of these are auric sight and mediumship.

It is scientifically estimated that at any given time within the range of our five senses, we are being bombarded by an estimate of 11 billion bits of information per second, of which we are only capable of processing between 50 and 300 bits per second, at the conscious level. The range described through research is broad; however, the one thing agreed upon is that it is ridiculously small compared to that which is perceived, and even more so to that which is actually happening in reality.

To put it into perspective, imagine you are holding your hands out, with palms facing up, and I dump 11 billion toothpicks out of a bag into them. The amount of toothpicks that would stay in your hands would be an estimate of 250, which represents the amount of information you can process at the conscious level—that is, if you had seven hours of restorative sleep and you didn't skip your morning coffee.

The experience of taking in reality is personal, selective, and limited. It is much like the experience of trying a new restaurant with friends. One person will always comment on the prices, another one on menu items and the variety or lack of, while someone else might focus on the ambiance, the music, and/or the service. Some will love it and come back; others would never recommend it.

Can you start to grasp how "let's agree to disagree" can be a powerful conflict resolution strategy? If the person you thought of at the beginning of the chapter is only holding 200 toothpicks in their hands, and you are holding a different set of 200 toothpicks out of the 11 million toothpicks that happened at the time of the situation you argued upon, then perhaps time and energy could be better spent upon discovering how many toothpicks you agree upon instead of pointing out the differences.

Or perhaps this new perspective has left you wondering if it is better to drop the toothpicks altogether and just move on.

Visit my website for fascinating resources on conflict resolution.

THE EGO SELF

We are often at fault for sabotaging our own goals, getting caught up in our own heads, and believing the limiting decisions we make about ourselves. When your ego goes on a power trip, you can easily fall under the spell of either victimhood or dictatorship, expecting the whole world to revolve around you.

The spell usually fades quickly away in a moment of contrast when someone points out your bad attitude, or when you encounter your own mirror image in someone else.

No matter how lovingly someone can help you see the ego act, such an experience often comes sprinkled with shame, guilt, and the feeling that you want to dig a hole and hide. But if these experiences were to happen more often, you would get out of your head faster. You would get over yourself and make action a priority over the paralyzing perfection that keeps telling you *nothing is ever good enough*.

Let me give you an example. As a breakthrough guide for my clients, it is part of my job to call them out when their ego has taken over, and to help them see a way of being that no longer serves them. It usually comes down to three scenarios: 1. Pointing out when they are telling me the same stuck story over and over again and are leaking energy by being stuck in a loop; 2. They are applying a judgement to another person, based on their own constructed reality; 3. They have been swimming a little too long in a negative emotion that no longer serves a purpose.

Once they can bring the situation into the light of their personal awareness, I guide them through a set of questions, much like this: What did you learn about yourself from this situation? What was the payoff for this way of being that got you to hold on to that for so long? How could you reinvent yourself and behave differently, if you were to encounter a similar set of circumstances in the future?

My clients often express that they experience a sense of lightness and empowerment in figuring out how much energy they were wasting without even realizing it. I lovingly encourage them not to dwell on wronging themselves but to instead create new actionable ways of being, to avoid bringing the past into the future.

Another key to embracing change with personal power and purpose is to create a new future instead of reenacting the past. This is also a fundamental tool to breaking bad habits, which is simply the past reincarnated in the future, over and over again.

The *ego self* is a part of the conscious mind that likes to be in control of things and loves certainties. It thrives on self-righteousness, and it loves to be fed with attention. The ego, in spite of being a troublemaker, is not necessarily your enemy. To say that it is good or bad is to throw a quick label on it without further investigation.

Contrary to the opinion of many, the ego is not an aspect of the self to get rid of, at least not for the average person living in the 21st century, who has a family, bills to pay, and is searching for meaning and purpose in life. In fact, it may very well be the aspect of the self in charge of creating contrasts so that you can continue to discern what is in line with your personal values and what isn't.

The ego is also connected to the aspect of yourself that makes you, different than me, and that cares about infusing life into things that matter to you specifically, and which possibly wouldn't matter in this life if you didn't exist.

The ego becomes an issue when it is out of balance and takes off on a power trip that has you holding grudges and fighting with others to be right rather than being happy. It turns out that the interactions with your fellow humans are the best way to get to know and work on balancing this aspect of yourself.

What the ego truly represents is the moment of highest contrast between the needs of the self and the giving of yourself to others.

One of the simplest and most powerful exercises you can do to keep your ego in check is to notice anytime there are conflicting emotions in your interactions with another person. Stop for a second and ask yourself, "Is what I am about to do or say out of love or out of ego?" If your answer is *ego,* the follow-up questions would be, "If I was acting out of love, what would I do and what would I say instead?"

Next time this happens—and even if you took a course of action that brought guilt or shame afterwards—be gentle with yourself. You don't know what you don't know, and that is why you need others to help you see that.

In the case of learning to master your ego, knowledge and meditation are the equivalent to sitting in a virtual reality training room. You still need to go out in the world and pass the true ego tests by interacting with others. Your family and friends, and even strangers and those you consider to be your enemies, can be the best teachers for learning to balance your ego self.

Be thankful for the circumstances or people that continuously provide opportunities to see yourself in a different light, because this makes you grow a lot faster than any course or book that teaches you about the ego. Sometimes the person that continually pisses you off the most is the person that holds the greatest opportunity for you to grow.

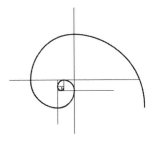

CHAPTER 5
DIGESTING REALITY

THE ALL-YOU-CAN-EAT REALITY BUFFET

Reality is a lot like an all-you-can-eat-buffet, but your experience of reality is like the two or three-plate servings you can handle, which are different than the six plates that the bodybuilder at the table next to you managed to eat, or the one plate barely touched by the uncomfortable woman behind you, who appeared to be on a date.

Reality is as personal as what you choose to put on your plate, and as personal as what you are able to digest.

Remember the toothpick analogy of 11 million bits of information per second exploding all around you, compared to the small amount of 300 bits that you manage to chew on? If you can grasp what this means, it is certain to make you feel like you are missing out on the all-you-can-eat reality buffet at times.

The same way your stomach can expand to be able to eat larger food portions, you are also capable of expanding the flexible limits of your window of reality intake. Whether by choice or as a default of change, the new experiences you are constantly being exposed to bring you the opportunity to expand your window of intake, and to grow into new levels of consciousness, one of the goals of those who seek to awaken and expand their minds and souls.

You do not need to worry about missing out on some of the delicious chunks that reality has to offer, as one of the functions of the unconscious mind is to accurately record everything within your sensory perception. Rest assured, the best treats reality can offer are safely stored within the fridges of your mind.

In a manner similar to the digestive system, your mind has a built-in mechanism that prevents you from experiencing reality indigestion. The mind itself is a funnel valve that assists you with processing the concept of infinity by chunking it down into linear and measurable meals. Reality, in terms of human consciousness, is served in three main courses: space, time, and matter, the preferred three-dimensional meals of human consciousness.

Once past the initial filters that digest reality into three-dimensional, the 300 bits of information move on to another set of personal filters. *Delete*, *distort*, and *generalize information* are three strategies used by your mind to distill the nutrients from reality that are of utmost relevance to you, so that you can efficiently interact with your environment during your conscious waking state.

Many thousands of years ago, the combined used of these filters were part of the survival mechanism that kept our ancestors alive. The stripes of a tiger that is hiding behind tall grass, perhaps cannot be assumed by a zebra to be a predator, but to a human whose mind has the ability to fill in the blanks and see the shape of a tiger, which would otherwise merge with the background, the assumption screams STAY AWAY!

Nowadays, you do not have to worry about a tiger stalking you behind tall grass; but just like the ego, when these filters run unchecked, they might be at cause for the glitches in the system that make you feel stuck.

At this very moment, as you read the information contained in these pages, the three filters are at play. At the unconscious level, everything you are reading is being recorded, letter by letter, and it is possible that under hypnosis, you could tell me exactly what you read on page 23, paragraph 3, 2nd line. But at the conscious level, your mind is deleting information that does not apply to you, distorting the meaning of my words according to what they personally mean to you, and making the generalization that this book reminds you of *that other book* you read.

Making assumptions, judgements, and jumping to conclusions, are glitches that happen in fractions of a second. It is of no major consequence when they happen as you read a book or watch TV in the safety and comfort of your own home. But when making assumptions, judgements, and jumping to conclusions is the cause of a family argument that lasts for years, it is worth taking a step back and evaluating if your reality filters need a little cleaning.

Deleting, distorting, and generalizing are often at fault for creating illusionary reenactments of the past, blurring your vision when it comes to taking in a new experience. In other words, bringing the shit from the past and superimposing it on a fresh, new experience happening in the clean "now."

It is definitely a lot safer to go to a restaurant where you know the type of service you will get. The reason your personal filters work so hard at digesting reality is because you can feel more in control, being under the illusion that you understand the dish that is about to be served at your table.

Let me remind you that it is human nature to prefer the certainty of familiar territory, rather than willingly leaping into change and being excited about conquering new experiences, which is a lot like eating something when you don't even know what it is.

The next section will give you a new frame of reference to make it possible for you to be excited tasting new reality dishes.

Are you ready for dessert?

HOW TO EAT CAKE

What is your mood like today? Does life appear to you as if you are looking at a glass half empty or half full, or is it so full of the wrong stuff that you feel like you are drowning more often than not? This is often referred to as *mood*.

Would your mood change if I knocked on your door and delivered the most beautiful cake, made of your favorite ingredients? My mood certainly changes when someone mentions dessert, no matter the day of the week or the time of the day. Desserts always brighten my day!

Mood swings are referred to as the subtle or major emotional fluctuations you experience based on what your sensory channels are feeding your mind. You can process the feeling of waking up with an achy lower back, which will in turn make your mood go awry. In this case, you know the cause of this particular emotional discomfort.

However, there are other instances where you are just feeling like the Grinch for no apparent reason. Because your unconscious mind accurately records everything within sensory perception—and not only that, it takes the information very personally—what you read on Facebook before getting out of bed, the weather and the horrible news you hear on the TV while you make breakfast in the kitchen, can unconsciously add up to a boiling point and wreck your mood too. The difference in this case is that you might not necessarily be able to pinpoint the source of your emotional distress.

The dialogue between your inner and outer world spirals out of control through irresponsible self-talk. In doing so, self-talk perpetuates more of the same emotional reality: great when it's good; but when it's bad, it's a lot like a train that is about to derail.

Now, remember that in Chapter 3, "Secrets of Successful Shapeshifters," I provided you with five strategies to assist you in changing the course of your day for the best. It is a matter of taking responsibility for the world inside of you. More resources can be found on my website. I love solving the puzzles of what my clients call "problems," and laying out a breadcrumb trail for them so that they may find their own perfect answers.

For a moment, I would like you to be aware of the part of you that is in charge of self-talk. This is the part that is reading these words out loud in your head. Can you hear it? Did it just answer yes or no, or at the moment is wondering what the hell this book is saying about a "voice in my head?" If you got what I am playing at, you are probably laughing right now, or you might be saying to yourself, "I am so confused right now."

Let's talk a bit more about this part of you. This part of you spearheads another set of filters that impact your intake of reality. These filters are your values, beliefs, language, memories and past frames of reference, decisions you have made about what time, energy, matter, and space mean, and so much more. The purpose of these filters is to continue to make sense of the world, and to continue digesting it to your needs so that you can be a functional human within a global society that is filled with a lot of collective rules and regulations. This part is often in the act of playing out back and forth conversations with yourself, constantly challenging, labeling, and assessing what is being perceived, and carrying on arguments with other people but *inside your head.*

Next time you are presented with a delicious dessert and you start hearing the voice in your head telling you to eat it, which then starts an argument with the other voice in your head listing the reasons why you shouldn't eat it, you are also going to laugh. You will have successfully become the observer of your "self-talk."

Energy in Motion

THIS IS FRUIT LOOPS

You have become more aware of your "self-talk" now and learned of three different layers of filtering systems: the infinity valve; delete, distort, and generalize; and the cluster of personal decisions. I can sense that you could start getting lost in understanding the complex filtering system that happens in milliseconds as you experience reality, and so I made a *Quick Access Reality Diagram* to help you look at the bigger picture. You can find it in the *Resources* section of my website.

Remember, whether it is with pictures or with words, as humans, we are simply attempting to grasp something that is infinite; we are attempting to understand the recipe of that which just *is* and has *no name*. To put it in other words, it is like using a tablespoon to scoop the sea up, one spoonful at a time, to put it in our own little beach buckets.

Not only do we perceive an insignificant chunk of reality compared to the whole, we filter it through our "personal stuff," and we also seem to fail terribly at recalling it with accuracy, according to recent studies in memory recall. In fact, most of what we perceive is a projection of our own selves and our past experiences anyway.

But it is indeed part of the human conscious experience to name things and, by naming them, make them part of our inner world. If we can name it, it means we can grasp it; however, more often than not, the reality cake we baked and ate tastes delicious in the moment, but it is certain to cause an upset stomach later on when we encounter a reality check.

How are we so paradoxically dissonant? Are we doomed to feel burdened by the understanding of the workings of being? Because it seems that the deeper we go, the more questions arise, to the point of driving anyone "fruit loops." Are we a failed experiment from an alien race, condemned to finish a puzzle with missing pieces?

If you happen to be a fan of conspiracy theories, you are very familiar with the reasons a government would "try to protect" their people from a mind-blowing discovery. *Truth* challenges the current state of reality. An exorbitant amount of newness causes discomfort, unrest, and conflict more often than not. On a global scale, it means volatile markets, monetary losses, and perhaps even war.

There is a passage in the Bible that narrates the story of what happened to Abraham after he saw "the tail of God's mantle." The poor man was so overwhelmed that he walked with a blindfold for 10 years, and after he could no longer remember what he saw, he felt troubled and shamed himself.

Perhaps eating a multilayered cake, one spoonful at a time, is just the perfect dose of truth that humans can handle.

This book is sure to give you a look at a 10-layer cake. I want to reassure you that even if you walk away from this experience by having tasted one spoonful from each layer, and then you can take a step back and look at the cake as a whole in relationship to your life, you are already ahead of 80% of the population of this planet.

MIND YOUR MOUTH

Words are the code of creation within human consciousness. An idea remains a ghost of a possible reality unless it somehow reaches the physical world. The first hint of an idea coming to life is usually someone's ability to put it into words. This is one of the most powerful uses of language. Language does not only describe; it is a tool with the capacity to create.

This high-level, intellectual, and cognitive function of the human race, however, can also play one hell of a prank on us.

As language usually finds its way out of your mouth as it is being created, it is often a reflection of the conscious and unconscious world within you—personal filtering systems of reality, and unresolved conflicts of your being. The Freudian term, *slip of tongue*, is used to describe something said by mistake, but it is regarded as a reflection of an unconscious or unrealized belief, thought, wish, or motive.

Arguably, some mistakes are simple distractions and have nothing to do with unresolved dark secrets from the swampy depths of your being. However, there are two specific phrases I would like you to be mindful of, especially when they come out of your own mouth. This practice will help you become more mindful in assessing if your own coachability index is running on low in the face of new and challenging ideas, and to be in constant practice of being at cause.

Number 1: The "I Know" Anthem

"I know" is the fastest way to command your subconscious mind to stop learning. "I know" means that your knowledge, or teachability cup, is full. So if you "know," what else is there to learn? To state the words is to command your mind to not know anymore. To the person attempting to share with you a piece of knowledge, it functions a lot like a subliminal message, saying that you are no longer able to listen to new ideas being presented.

To *know* and not *do* is really not to know. If you truly knew, then why would you be seeking advice? The physical manifestation of knowledge is the irrefutable, ultimate proof that you know. If you ain't got it, then you don't really, really know it.

If you catch yourself singing the "I know" anthem, stop and rephrase to "I acknowledge or I am aware; I have not put it into practice yet but am now learning how to," or anything similar that resonates with you. This will send the message to your mind to continue learning and seek opportunities to take action, and might even connect you with the perfect teacher.

Number 2: The "But" Wall

The word "but" very much functions like a border between countries, especially when it comes paired with an apology.

"I am sorry I was such an ass to you, but you just drive me mad every time you…"

The apology is there; that is, until the word "but" came to put up a wall and leave it behind to then list back all the faults of the person receiving the apology.

I can also hear the "but" wall when a client is unaccepting of a piece of advice, much like the "I know" anthem.

"Yes, I know I have to take my time to acknowledge the food I am eating, but most of the time, I am at the office and…"

I usually take it as a sign that what I think is the perfect answer, is not perfect for them at that moment, even though the client might have asked for my solution to their problem. As a mind guide, I then shift into leading them to find their own solution. But not everyone out there has the vision to shift into higher coaching states, or to help the person become aware that they are reinforcing their own roadblock.

As long as you, or someone, can catch you in the act, you are in the running for experiencing an awakening. It starts with being aware of something that you previously were not. And so I will now challenge you to explore how you have been practicing hypnosis every day without even knowing you were, and what the benefits are to bringing this into the light of your awareness.

SELF-HYPNOSIS

Much like the word *unconscious*, the term *hypnosis* is wrongly attributed to a state where an individual loses their sense of self, and therefore loses control over his or her conscious waking state.

When a person finds out that I am a hypnotherapist, to my amusement, they immediately take a step away from me, elevate their tone of voice, and half-jokingly or maybe half-accusingly, ask, "Are you hypnotizing me right now?"

Contrary to false advertising and popular belief, hypnosis is simply a label for a natural state of relaxation, where anyone can experience states of consciousness that vary in depth. In fact, reading a book and scrolling through Instagram are mild hypnotic states that you are used to experiencing on a daily basis. Other examples of everyday circumstances that cause you to experience mild states of hypnosis are: listening to music that you love, having a deep conversation with a peer, focusing on your breathing, cooking, doing a weightlifting session mindfully, sleeping, driving, etc.

So, the answer to the question in paragraph two, technically, is "Yes, I was hypnotizing you when you decided to give me your undivided attention in a conversation that seemed important to you, until you broke rapport with me when you heard the word *hypnosis,* and you decided to get all caught up in your head (your self-hypnosis, also self-talk) when your amygdala triggered a survival mechanism, fearing that I might have started to control you as a puppet, right here and now, in the middle of this lovely party where we are both drinking a beer."

Here is a joke for you. You might even laugh if you are really getting what this self-hypnosis is all about. What is the difference between a yoga teacher, a math teacher, and a hypnotherapist? One can bend like a pretzel while the other two can't, but the three of them can hypnotize you.

Hypnosis can be generated by yourself or through the interaction with a person, object, or setting.

Meditation is the most common consciously practiced form of self-hypnosis. The effect that listening to the news has on you, as well as how you feel after scrolling through social media, are the most common forms of practicing hypnosis through the interaction of an external feedback system, which when used unaware and irresponsibly, leave you having all sorts of emotional mood swings.

As you can see, it is in your best interest that you learn more about hypnosis, but in order to do so, I am going to ask you to see past the label that either creates mysticism, glorifies the practice, or has a person fearing that they might start walking on all fours and barking like a dog without their consent.

A definite prerequisite for any form of hypnosis is consent and rapport. This is thanks to the marvelous job your unconscious mind faithfully executes as a guardian of the integrity of your consciousness. You would not have been able to make it this far into *Energy in Motion* if the information contained did not resonate with you. That is an example of rapport.

If you are by yourself at home and just binge watched five episodes of your favorite Netflix show, no one forced you into that hypnotic state; you chose to sit through it. This is an example of consent, and even though you consented with yourself to start watching the show, had you gotten a headache in the first 30 minutes, that would have broken rapport with the state of watching TV, and you would have decided to take Advil and take a nap instead. Hypnosis, with anything, works the same way.

The most important form of hypnosis that I would like you to start getting very familiar with is your *self-talk*. You have the power inside yourself to talk yourself into and out of things faster than anything else.

Good self-talk is great when it assists you in bravely reaching new heights in taking purposeful action toward your goals and dreams, but it can get addictive to the point that it allows the ego to step all over others around you.

For some people, self-talk is unbearable, as it carries the nostalgic notes of forgotten dreams, and the hateful words of deeply buried, self-loathing and troubling questions that have no answers. When the self-talk gets loud, and not in a good way, the most common responses are to avoid it by paying attention to any other noise rather than hearing the inner voice, and numbing it with the use of alcohol, substances, and anything that is addictive enough to make the person forget what they are hearing.

Lifelong self-talk avoidance adds up to a heavy baggage of pain that a person may carry for the rest of their lives.

Give yourself permission to listen to your self-talk. Your unconscious mind sends messages through it, sometimes of the unfinished business you have with yourself. Start writing in your journal or stating out loud: "I give myself permission to listen and learn from my self-talk." Make note of important and reoccurring words and how they make you feel.

The next two chapters will gift you with the ability to decode the energy of your emotions and find the answers that you have forgotten you needed to know the most.

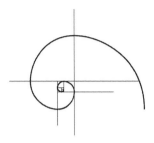

CHAPTER 6
ENERGY IN MOTION

THE IGNITION KEY

> *"What is this spark that ignites motion,*
> *the flame that follows, and uncontrolled*
> *the overwhelming wildfire that consumes us…"*

~ excerpt from "The Spark" poem, by Alejandra Díaz Mercado

There is an undeniable energy, a life force, palpitating inside every single heart, atom, cell, brain, plant, insect—pretty much anything on this planet, and even the planet itself. Absolutely everything in this Universe is always up to something—to exist, grow, replicate, reproduce, move, evolve, improve… to be something, do something, have something… to be unstoppable, inevitable, incorruptible—yet is capable of being redirected and even reinvented. Everything is in constant expansion and in constant motion.

Your body holds inside, a droplet of the magnificent and infinite force that is expanding that Universe. That droplet is the spark of life.

The spark of life is mysteriously ignited around the 18th day of a human's gestational period, compelling the human heart to deliver blood to all other tissues. Without this spark, human life is not possible.

What is that spark? Where did it come from?

Many historians and poets claim that love is the force that creates life, moves mountains, and inspires the human spirit to experience life on Earth. Other less popular theories speculate as to

Energy in Motion

the power of hate. The multibillion-dollar franchise of *Star Wars* actually calls it "the Force," and has been quite successful in capturing the archetypical dance between its opposites, Zen and fear, love and hate.

With the dawn of human consciousness came the realization that the forces of good and evil, life and death, right and left, interact in a complex choreography that permeates the very own fabric of our perceived reality. From the smallest blade of glass to the farthest known galaxy, all are ruled by this law of opposites, in a ballet of ebbs and flows and ups and downs, like the waves in an endless ocean. It sometimes seems that we are but a boat trying to navigate in the midst of that enormity, wondering if we know where we are going, or how we got there in the first place.

Even this book that you are holding in your hands, somehow contains a droplet of this *energy*. Remember that even if it is back on the shelf, it is still rotating in an orbit around the sun, in a Universe that as far as we know is still expanding.

Despite the fact that you and I keep forgetting the certainty that Earth continues to rotate around the sun, curiosity gets the best of us all the time. And this is the reason why, in this day and age, we have no shortage of disciplines from which to choose our preferred method of studying and understanding this magnificent *force* and all of its variables.

What do you prefer? Do you like to dig in the past for answers, stay grounded in the present, or focus on the possibilities that lie in the future? Do you prefer a scientific or ethereal approach? Do you like your studies structured or free flowing?

Religion, medicine, psychology, yoga, future studies, mathematics, arts, quantum physics, hypnosis—you name it; we have an incredible selection of flavors, all of which study fundamental questions that relate to this *force*: Where does it come from? What can we do with it? How does it work? Why are we here? Where are we going? Etc., etc....

But let's focus on you, because perhaps the most important thing in your life right now is just figuring out how to get through this week, or even just through today.

TO EMBODY THE FORCE

If instinct alone got you out of bed in the mornings, you would probably occupy all your time and energy in the day to eat, reproduce, sleep it off, and do it all over again. The human race indeed spent thousands of years doing that already, and so, generally speaking, has outgrown that developmental stage and moved on to bigger and better things. Like I said, generally speaking...

Among those things is the quest to understand this magnificent *force* that moves us, despite the fact that it seems to go dormant in the presence of pizza and Netflix. You will learn more about why that happens, in Chapter 8, "Human Problems, Destructive Abundance."

When this powerful *force* is in action, its magnitude can fuel a single mother with three children to work two jobs while still caring for her family, and a child to survive an encounter with cancer—and certainly gave my grandfather the strength to remain so stubborn until the last day of his life.

Place both of your hands on your chest or the sides of your neck, and feel the beating presence of your very own life force. When was the last time you took a moment to acknowledge it? Just take 10 seconds right now to connect with your own life force. Without it, you cannot be you, you cannot live, and you cannot be here.

But I know that along with this knowing, you also have a feeling of restlessness inside of you, a sense of incompletion and so many buried questions. It is uncomfortable, and a lot of people spend their adulthood chasing external feedback to avoid the inner silence where these ghosts live, or where the ugly self-talk never stops.

This is a collective human experience. It is as if we were cursed to feel the *force* but be unable to fully grasp it, and therefore be left with just small traces of its power, wandering around in circles, looking for answers or avoiding asking the questions.

Unfortunately, our societal structures and education systems are built in complete avoidance of the experience of the obvious, the discomfort of feeling this power, and the discomfort of letting ourselves feel human emotions. And instead of being "human beings," we become "human doings," doing all sorts of things that have us disassociated from who we really are. Lacking in the understanding of what emotions are and how to use them, leaves a person feeling powerless and at the mercy of whatever emotions and circumstances haphazardly show up to control their lives.

It is time for some answers. It's time to understand that you are the master of such power, and not the other way around.

Emotions are precisely these traces of the *force* I am referring to, and despite being so aware that you have them, you might not know where to put them, when to show or hide them, nor how to use them. But if you think about it for a second, after having covered your basic survival needs, and without any sort of emotion, is there really an incentive to do anything in this life?

Emotions are the energy of life itself. An emotion is an energy inside of you, with the purpose to get you moving out and about in the world. Emotions are the whispers that come from Life Source.

Emotions are also the domain of the unconscious mind; and guess what? That is why no matter how hard you try to feel a certain way, it takes a lot of effort to deny how you truly feel. To do so is to try in vain to ignore what your unconscious mind wants you to know; to do so is to try to fight the 90% of your mind (unconscious mind) with the 10% of your mind (conscious mind). That is why it takes pages and pages of positive affirmations, which go up in flames the next time you hit your toe on the edge of the sofa. That is why the "think positive" attitude is but a temporary Band Aid on an unclean wound.

Emotions are your access key to unleashing the power of 90% of your mind. Are you ready to learn more about them now?

EMOTIONS

> *"The energy that moves a thought across your mind is the same energy that moves a star across the sky."*
> ~ Wayne Dyer

You can hug a person who is sad, or look at a painting of a very angry artist, or hear the insults of someone mad with rage. You can feel your chest perk up with happiness, or your shoulders drop down with a burden you've carried for a long time, but you cannot touch an emotion. You can only feel it and perceive the effect it has on the world around you.

Energy in Motion

An emotion is a form of energy that can only be generated inside a human being. It comes as a result of or in response to an internal or external experience or a thought. It is the energy that fuels the need to do something, be something, or have something. It always has or serves a purpose, and this is precisely the reason why intense emotions make you do things you don't want to sometimes, like eating a liter of ice-cream on a sad Saturday night!

The more intense an emotion, the more obvious the physical manifestation of it will be, both to the person experiencing it and to those perceiving it.

Psychology affects physiology, and because the body is also the domain of the unconscious mind, physiology ends up being an efficient source of nonverbal communication picked up by the unconscious minds of others. That is why sometimes you may dislike a person but you cannot justify why. A lot can be said without words; in fact, it is proven that more than 60% of human communication is nonverbal.

Furthermore, emotions also seem to have a vibrational quality that extends beyond the person generating them. Have you ever seen a whole room get a little brighter or a little darker when a specific person walked in? Unconscious minds seem to be fantastic at picking up on what we call "vibes," a slang word for the vibration being exuded past the physical body of someone experiencing an emotion.

Emotions, as such, are contagious. Negative emotions, unfortunately, seem to spread a lot faster than positive ones—just observe road rage as a social experiment.

But it only takes one awakened mind to stop the ripple effect of negativity. That is another reason why this book was created: to bring to light the power you have, not just in your life when learning more about the use of emotions, but the magnificent ripple effect you can cause in the complex tapestry of humanity. When you feel just a little bit better, you win, and the whole Universe wins too.

Back in the personal gains department, I want to share with you why emotions are so popular when it comes to the "law of attraction" and the power to manifest whatever you want in your life. I will not try to convince you that you can attract anything you want into your life, but I instead want to point out the logical and the obvious as to why this happens.

You exist in the "now"—agreed? And the "now" is a collection of "nows" that are constantly happening. The moment a "now" passes, it then becomes the past, but you have the power to bring the past back to life by recalling any one specific moment in the past, and reliving in your body through the imaginative activation of your five senses. Connecting with the emotion that was present during that time is the last ingredient that binds the spell.

This is the foundation upon which the "Shapeshifting for Beginners" exercise, which you learned in Chapter 3, was created. This is also the basis for understanding key elements in PTSD. When a past memory, stored in the mind, is activated by reliving it with the five senses and the emotions that were present at that time, the past comes to life in the "now." And so the past can feel as real as if it were happening all over again. Emotion is the energy that infuses life to a memory; emotion is the life force that can bring back the ghosts from the past.

When it comes to the future, emotion is the energy that gives life to your goals. It is actually the power to create a self-fulfilling prophecy. In other words, you can use your five senses to create with your imagination what you want to experience in the future, and then infuse it with life through emotion. If you, for a moment, recall how everything you do in your life is fueled by an emotion that serves a purpose—for example, providing for your family, being a better spouse, making your parents proud, etc.—you will realize that the art of manifesting is not a magic trick; it is actually the conscious awareness of where you want to place your time, energy, mind, thoughts, and plans, fueled by the emotion to succeed in that purpose.

For example, if one of your current missions is to be a good spouse, why would you have an online profile on a dating app? That would just be an absolute tug of war when it comes to achieving the purpose of being a good spouse. But hey, I get that humans press the self-sabotage button quite often, and the cause might actually be some deeply buried negative emotions or limiting decisions a person is dragging around from a distant past. The good thing is that we are going to take a full dive into the purpose of those heavy things, in Chapter 7.

An emotion is an energy with a purpose. It is an energy that fuels you to take action, redirect course, or stop altogether when you are headed for the self-sabotage button.

Most often than not, emotions are like separate instruments in an orchestra, playing their own dissonant tunes. Your mind is the orchestra director, and when you take ownership over that power and responsibility, you can elegantly compel those instruments to tune up and play a beautiful and coherent harmony, for yourself and those you love.

SOURCE AND PURPOSE

*"Above all else, guard your heart,
for everything you do flows from it."*
~ Proverbs 4:23

Perhaps it is due to the undeniable feeling of the change in our heartbeat when we are about to speak in public, or when we spot our crush, or get scared by a really good horror movie, that has us thinking that the heart is the center of emotions.

Just like we attribute the brain with housing our mind, we literally take it to heart when it comes to emotions.

The heart is indeed a fascinating miracle of life, and there are several facts about it worth remembering.

The first heartbeat in a human gets ignited around day 18–21 after conception. A cluster of cells mysteriously start generating their own electrical signals, and beating synchronically, even before the heart is fully formed. These cells will cluster into what shortly is to become the Sinoatrial Node, the *spark plug of life*, which will signal a more developed heart to pump the nurturing flow of blood, and therefore life, into the newly formed fetal organs. Without a heartbeat, life cannot enter the body.

Scientists have been able to spark life into isolated heart cells on a petri dish, but what they haven't been able to do yet is to get them beating in a synchronized manner. Humanity still has not cracked the code to what it is that enables human life to enter the body. Maybe that is a blessing, or maybe that is a curse.

As of now, anything that we think happens in between lifeless and living, is mere speculation.

But what is certain is that you carry the force of life in your heart. Many ancient cultures worshiped the human heart as the most important organ in the body, and it wasn't until the Scientific Revolution that we turned our attention to the worship of the brain as the center of the human Universe.

But it is neither in the heart nor in the brain that we feel emotions. If you have been doing your share of self-knowledge work, you would have noticed that you actually feel emotions in different parts of your body.

For example, most people describe feeling anger in the pit of their stomach, stress in their neck and shoulders, and overwhelm in the head. It is also worth mentioning that sayings make use of colors to describe emotional flare ups, such as "green with envy," "red with rage," and "I've got the blues." If you have ever caught yourself in the middle of an intense emotion, you might also have experienced that it has a certain vibration or energetic impact in your body as well. A clear example is the exhaustion you feel after getting into a screaming fight with a loved one.

Furthermore, you might have heard how an emotion that "gets stuck" inside the body for too long might be the cause of certain illnesses. There are various studies that have linked an intense emotional experience to the development of cancer within a three to five-year period. I am not asking you to believe this, but instead, if you feel this has piqued your interest, I encourage you to conduct your personal research on the matter.

The specific reason why this is worth mentioning here is because all signs point to the mind, body, and spirit benefits that you can have by understanding the source and purpose of your emotions. Not only that, there is true power yet to be harnessed by understanding emotions as a form of energetic vibration.

In recent years, various disciplines have redirected their focus to emotions, heart coherence, and emotional intelligence for a reason.

One of the missions of this book is to encourage you to look at emotions in practical terms, and the personal benefits you can obtain in your life, and extend them to those you love by doing so. Emotions are very much like a compass that you can learn how to read, and their purpose is to point you in the precise direction an action must be taken, especially when there is a sense of incompletion or discomfort when looking at that direction in light of your awareness.

There is indeed something sacred surrounding that heart space within us that holds a key to understanding life's purpose. Figuratively speaking, if brain is mind, heart is probably closer to soul, for something cannot exist without a heart in it.

EMOTIONAL VIBES

I once heard an ancient tale about the reason certain souls chose to come to Earth to have a human experience. According to this particular tale, this was the only way a soul could experience and learn what emotions meant.

Emotions, much like the five senses, have the purpose of helping our minds expand in awareness. All the emotions you are capable of feeling are much like all the colors you are able to see. Your experience of reality would be a lot narrower if you were unable to feel one less of those emotions. Throughout your life, your emotional color perception will continue to deepen in light of understanding new layers of what it means to be a human being.

Contrast is a tool that allows you to assess where you stand in the vastness of the emotional spectrum. Without it, you wouldn't be able to know if you are in a higher and more creative vibrational state, or in a lower and more stagnant one. With this statement, I do not mean to imply that if you haven't had your share of blacks and dark greys compared to other people, you should go out and seek to stain your pastel-colored painting. Not at all! This simply means that you are more likely to be a better human and do more with your life if you are happy, than if you are upset.

The consequences of walking around with a heavy baggage of dark emotions can be devastating for yourself and others. If you feel you need some real life examples, all you have to do is turn on the news channel. But don't do that right now; it is my mission to elevate your vibration and keep your attention in matters that will do that for you.

The sense that allows you to perceive emotions exists inside of you in connection with your body, and perhaps it doesn't have a name yet, but it is an actual sense. You are very familiar with the feeling of a heightened heart rate and the heat that expands inside of you when you get angry, versus the weakness you feel all over when you are saddened. This is the energy I am referring to; it is an actual physiological experience, and when I refer to emotional vibration, I am referring to the difference in the effect of the active versus passive energy that you are able to perceive inside of you.

The vibrational quality of an emotion holds information as to what could possibly be the purpose for having that particular emotion. For example, the vibrational quality of excitement might serve the purpose of preparing your body for a ping pong match, whereas the vibrational quality of anger might serve the purpose of assertively shouting at someone who is trespassing on a personal boundary. Excitement and anger are two emotions with an active energy wavelength, but which serve two very different purposes.

The vibrational scale of emotions is very much like a ladder, where emotions of similar energy or vibration can be found next to each other. This makes it possible for anyone to easily access an emotion that makes you feel just a little bit better, and to climb up that ladder.

It is also possible to do emotional quantum leaps, and you can access an exercise, on my website, called "Taking Your First Emotional Quantum Leap."

Even though changing into a higher vibrational state or emotion is simply a matter of choosing to do it, I understand that there are moments in life where this proposal sounds completely ludicrous. Several years ago, I experienced a profound and paralyzing depression that lasted more than a year, and I would have likely punched in the face anyone who had told me that happiness and well-being was a matter of choosing to "vibe higher."

What could have been useful for me to know during that year of suffocating darkness, was that being able to cry was already a sign of progress. But neither I nor the people around me understood negative emotions like we do now.

For some people, a deep state of depression, unfortunately, is only one step prior to ending their lives. Depression is such a low vibrating energy that its wavelength is almost flat—metaphorically speaking, almost like the monitor's flat line when the heart stops beating. And that is why I cannot stress enough the importance of any emotion that vibrates even slightly higher than depression, like sadness or hate or fear, because that will infuse some life into that flat line.

Going through my personal depression, and giving myself permission to acknowledge when I had negative emotions, allowed me to discover that negative emotions do have a purpose of the highest good.

Emotions are one of the ways your unconscious mind communicates with you. It certainly is one hell of a way to grab your attention while your conscious mind suffers from "squirrel syndrome," jumping from thought to thought and getting stressed about what to make for dinner tonight.

I am thankful for the year of darkness that I traveled, and I would not dare to change a single thing in my past; for I feel, without it, I could not have confidently written the chapter that is to follow, which has the purpose of helping you understand some of the darkest and less discussed negative emotions a human can experience.

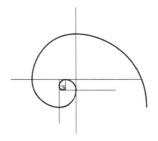

CHAPTER 7
THE ART OF SWIMMING IN THE DARK

UNDERSTANDING THE PURPOSE OF NEGATIVE EMOTIONS

Humans have come close to mastering the art of what to do with positive emotions: starting a new business, giving birth to a new life, and "moving mountains," just to name a few miraculous feats. But as of now, our species still proves to be relatively incompetent when it comes to finding purpose for negative emotions.

The favored strategies to deal with negative emotions include ignoring, rationalizing, and burying them, and putting the "think positive Band Aid" on an unclean wound.

That's right; trying the "thinking positive strategy," when there is an underlying cause, is as useless as putting a Band Aid on your hand after having been scratched by a cat, without cleaning the wound first. If you haven't dealt with the core issue, emotion, or limiting decision, no amount of thinking positive is going to make things better in the long run. In fact, to your detriment, you would be expending copious amounts of energy in trying, without much success, to feel better. It is a lot like playing tug of war and getting not too far ahead in one direction or another, and then getting so tired that all you end up doing is sitting down in the same spot you started, just to catch your breath.

The real problem arises when the pressure inside a person builds up to the point of an explosion of catastrophic proportions, like when road rage turns into a fatal accident, or when the wound is so painful or rotten that it completely shuts down a person from living a life with purpose, and turns into depression, drug use, and ultimately suicide as a way out. Another negative effect is when the body manifests the dis-ease of the mind and spirit as a fatal illness—not favorable scenarios either way.

Energy in Motion

If you need to find reasons to get proactive on personal and spiritual development, these are it.

There is true power to be claimed in the dominion of negative emotions, and in order to claim that power for yourself, there are two main requirements you'll need to meet: one, the willingness to go there; and two, the knowledge on what to do once you are there in the unexplored chambers of your psyche.

It is my hope that this book has helped you gain some new insights and has expanded your awareness into new territories. Awareness comes prior to the acquisition of new and useful knowledge. In light of this new awareness, you might have noticed that there are some very uncomfortable aspects of your psyche that you are not ready to look at, and also some new and playful aspects of your mind that might even feel like new superpowers you'd like to explore.

Remember, the human mind is like an unexplored mansion, full of dark rooms, and once in a while, you might enter a room full of dark creatures or objects you do not understand or seem scary. This is a great reason to have a mentor that knows more than you, and who you look up to that can guide you. Part of the problem with modern spirituality is that we want to do it all by ourselves, and when we come back with a new piece of information that we don't know what it is, it wreaks havoc in the familiar structures of our lives.

Part of my job as an unconscious mind guide with my clients is precisely to help them make sense of new information they have acquired in the journey of expansion, and how to integrate it, with flow and excitement, into their lives. They have often expressed how confusion and breakdowns have been prevented out of having me help them decode their newly acquired insights.

I currently work with a client who has tapped into a room where there are creatures she is not ready to look at. There is nothing wrong with acknowledging that one is not ready yet, as long as that choice is not stopping the person from living a creative and purposeful life. After getting some reassurance from me, she stopped wronging herself for it, and continues to live a beautiful life.

I am now going to challenge your willingness to look at some of these creatures with me. I will get to show some of the reframing work I do with my clients. In the following pages, I am going to guide your flashlight inside those rooms so that you can study some of the most familiar negative emotions, under a new light. It is under this new perspective that you will be able to obtain the learnings that these creatures may hold for you, so that you may find clarity as to what could be the purpose of those emotions for you.

Come on now; let us shine the light on those gremlins.

THE UNWARRANTED AND THE PURPOSEFUL

Living in a society so disconnected from emotions, one of the biggest self-knowledge superpowers you can start developing now is a vast vocabulary for naming emotions. Feeling "good," "bad," "okay," "upset," and "doing fine" is usually as far as most people's vocabulary goes.

My first challenge to you is to get a bit more creative next time you are with someone worth describing your current emotional state to. "Okay," "good," "not so bad," and your other go-tos are no longer acceptable. Challenge your emotional IQ by growing that vocabulary.

Energy in Motion

In previous pages, I discussed how an emotion is an energy with a purpose. When it comes to negative emotions, it is going to be of great use for you to discover if they belong to the purposeful family or the unwarranted gang.

The purposeful family of negative emotions will usually guide you into taking purposeful action. Action transforms the physical world, and this is the ultimate mission of an emotion: to become energy in motion through action. The purposeful family will work closely with your prefrontal cortex in helping you break the habit of being yourself, and create new and improved ways of being.

The unwarranted gang of negative emotions likes to hang out with the ego self, and is great friends with the amygdala. It will trick you into remaining stagnant and inactive in the face of discomfort and change. To know if a negative emotion belongs in the unwarranted gang, all you need to do is realize if it does not serve a purpose, or if you are getting an ego payoff by feeling that particular emotion. Two examples of a payoff are getting too much attention from the people around you, or procrastinating in having to make an important decision.

I am going to start by naming a cluster of five negative emotions that seem to work together to veil you from your ability to be at cause. Remember, to be at cause means that you are in full control of what happens inside of you, and of the actions you decide to take next. When you are stuck in any of these emotions, you are left powerless and at the effect side of things. If you find this particular behavioral pattern does not apply to you, you might still find it useful to learn of other ways you can look at these emotions the next time you experience them.

These five are: anger, sadness, fear, hurt, and guilt.

Anger is the utmost coat of this complex cluster, and functions as a shielding device, deflecting others from getting near you physically or psychologically, or both. In a purposeful state, anger serves to protect you against an unfair circumstance, but in an unwarranted state, it is the way of the ego to avoid even getting near the cause of the problem.

Sadness is the experience of becoming disarmed, and unconsciously connected to a state of surrender or defeat. Sadness is a very real emotion, and it usually arises out of a perceived loss or definite change. It can be similar to grief, yet grief is a true wild creature in its own right, and I will give it its own section further on. To make purposeful use of the energy of sadness, think of any activity that can be nurturing to you. Purposeful sadness might get you to reconnect with nature, write some beautiful poetry, or reach out for help to those who love you. Sadness turns unwarranted when the heart has not been nurtured, and you find yourself swimming in sadness a little too long, and eating bags and bags of chips; also, when the payoff is getting too much attention and avoiding fulfilling responsibilities.

Once the buckets of tears and sadness have been emptied, there is usually a feeling of emptiness and uncertainty. *Fear* is what humans are biologically wired to feel in the face of the unknown. It is then that the fight or flight response, or the need to be shielded again with anger, might arise; but because, for the most part, you are no longer experiencing the threat of wild animals or other tribes trying to kill you, after you get past the fear, you might incur feeling hurt. This emotion comes from erroneously perceiving yourself as a victim, and it is the ego's way of blaming others for what happens to you.

As you are getting closer to your power to be at cause for your circumstances, you might travel through the deepest layer of this cluster of five. At the core lies guilt, or what I call "creator's curse," and this is the erroneous belief that because you are at cause, then you are the one to blame for creating the painful circumstances around what has happened.

These five negative emotions, whether unwarranted or purposeful, each hold a valuable lesson. Dropping the shield of anger holds the key for your willingness to accept change, and be coachable and teachable by the circumstances. Allowing yourself to feel sadness enables you to connect with the human capabilities of empathy, vulnerability and compassion, and also lets others near you. You move past your fear when you are able to reconnect to your source of personal power and realize you have the strength and courage to overcome any circumstance. This goes hand in hand with not being a victim, and taking the reins of your mind again.

To move past guilt is to reclaim your power to be at cause in the realization that you get to choose how you feel and what action you are going to take next. Or in the instance that you believe you created the circumstances of the problem, you now know that you also have the power to undo them and completely redefine your reality.

Remember, emotions are how your unconscious mind communicates with you, so stop wronging yourself for being able to feel them. Instead, start paying attention to when and how they show up, and start becoming your own *emotions detective*. Now you know some of the signs that can help you conduct a deeper investigation to know whether a negative emotion is pointing you in the direction of a purposeful action, or if it belongs in the unwarranted gang.

WILD CREATURES OF THE DEEP DARK

Disclaimer: My intention with the following chapter is not to tell you how to handle some of these emotions, nor to redefine them. My intention is to share information contained within their vibrational quality, which I am able to decode, and in doing so, you might get to know a different side of them and make use of their energy to generate breakthroughs in your own life. Take what serves you, and disregard what doesn't resonate with you.

Envy, anxiety, rage, guilt, shame, worry, stress, depression, and grief are unwelcomed, scary, and perhaps even taboo emotions that we tend to hide in dark corners of our minds, like dirty little secrets. As I decode them for you, I invite you to make a mental or written note on any insights that apply to you and can help you in your journey to seek completion.

Envy is a mid to low vibration emotion that is usually felt toward another person. Interestingly enough, you can envy yourself; for example, you can envy the body you had in your early 20s. Most often than not, it catches you unawares, especially when you feel it toward someone you care about. Envy is an experience of contrast that might show you a personal desire or goal you have given up on. When you feel envy, you subconsciously feel that you have been cheated on or stolen from. It is an emotion that arises in the face of someone who accomplishes that which you consciously or subconsciously desire, but upon which you are not taking action on or decided to give up on. Envy is so specific to a person and circumstance that it can actually help you gain clarity in an area of your life that needs your attention. I have a story on my blog about the last time I felt envy toward one of my best friends.

Anxiety is a form of frantic, high vibrational energy, very similar to that of the excitement one might feel before bungee jumping or starting a 100m sprint. This form of high vibration energy had an original purpose of taking powerful action or making an important decision, but because this action was not taken, the energy became trapped inside the body. Even though it manifests in the present, it usually takes origin in the past, and grows more and more out of the accumulation of time without action.

Rage is boiling anger, to the point of an explosion of energy that vibrates uncontrollably at catastrophic proportions. It is like being possessed by an evil spirit on a killing spree. This metaphor is a fantastic way to understand why, in the midst of a raging fit, a part of you feels like the helpless observer of the other part of you that wreaks havoc with words and actions that you know you will most certainly regret later. Yet you are not able to stop yourself. Rage is completely avoidable by paying attention to the anger bombs that keep going off here and there. When there is a complete disregard for built-up anger, the purpose of rage is then to relieve pressure from the pressure cooker. Speculating, I might dare to say that without such relief, a person might be in danger of developing fatal heart disease or some form of cancer. These diseases are another reason why it's worth looking at the reoccurrence of anger or hate, and of course the rage explosions.

Guilt is like a ghost that follows a person around; it usually is of mid to low vibration in nature, and it gets heavier and heavier over time. It can eat away at someone in silence. It takes root in an incomplete past. It can be from an immediate past or a long time past. It is a sign that in some way or manner, the person feels responsible for the pain of others, or being at cause for a negative circumstance in their life. It wakes people up at night, sits next to them on the couch, and stands behind them during a conversation. Because it's a heavy burden and always seems to be around, a lot of people that feel it incur distracting or numbing activities, like drinking or watching too much TV. Guilt eventually becomes like a tight rope around the neck, thwarting a person's ability to move and breathe. This is a clear sign that the person's unconscious mind is seeking completion or redemption with something in their past. The circumstance, person, or matter is usually very clear, unless a person has numbed themselves down and cannot point in the direction the guilt is coming from. Guilt most often serves the purpose of surrendering and being able to verbalize, "I am sorry." Inaction evolves into feeling powerless. Guilt also prevents someone from repeating self-harming attitudes and behaviors, and gets people off their butts when they've have had too much ice-cream.

Depression is a low and dormant vibrational state. It can be foggy or dark. It can be accompanied by bouts of physical pain or complete numbness. The five senses are dulled, food loses its taste, and things literally look dull. The person might also experience a dissociation with their own body. This might explain why some people harm their bodies in order to feel something or to become associated again. The path back is to simply feel a little bit better. The simplicity of nature or the company of a pet can be a way of gently infusing life back. Crying might be useful in moving some energy too, and feeling something again.

Grief, much like depression, is an extremely deep sadness that arises out of a permanent change or loss, real or perceptual. It is primal, wild, and unpredictable. Its vibrational quality takes a person on a roller coaster ride of hell, from experiencing high frantic states of motion, to paralysis and all that is in between, without any sort of warning. Friends appear as enemies, and enemies appear as friends. Large chunks of a person's day go into the oblivion, unable to be recalled by the conscious memory. As grief progresses, reality seems to readjust itself and even take on a new meaning, sometimes making the person feel like they no longer belong. Because grief is so wild and unpredictable, it is very helpful to allow someone, who the person loves and trusts, to know that they are experiencing grief. In grief, someone is bound to fall apart into million pieces, so that with time they can reconstruct a new reality without that which has been lost. The road out of the personal labyrinth of grief is a personal and lonely journey.

Shame is a heavy burden to carry. It is a heavy energy that dims a person's light and crushes their spirit. The source is usually a discrepancy between the inner and outer world, an incoherence between the pure energy of a person and the unexplained gap between that energy and the restrictions imposed by sex, age, belief systems, society, etc. For example, there is a lot of shame surrounding sexuality due to the conflict a person might experience with the acceptance, without further investigation, of a societal, religious, or family belief that pertains to that subject. As so it can translate into the wronging of one's innocence by the impositions of a group. Shame can also arise as a result of being incomplete with a past experience, or out of a betrayal of a personal boundary such as physical abuse. Shame is the inability to speak the truth for fear of retaliation. Shame most often than not is purposeful because it calls the person to come to terms with a part of themselves that is perceived as aching or incomplete. Shame is only unwarranted in the context where the individual indulges in self-punishment, as a way to avoid courageously looking at the source of shame and/or seek completion. Shame can arise from trauma that was not dealt with. I can personally attest to the fact that courage of heroic proportions is needed to face personal shame.

Worry and *stress* are two emotions that arise from the irresponsible use of the power of imagination and focus. When you choose to imagine a possible future that has not yet come to pass, you are investing your energy into it from the "now," but instead of getting a return, you begin to sink in energy debt. That debt triggers fear and survival mechanisms, flooding your body with stress hormones in the face of an illusion. Those chemicals get trapped inside your body. Not only is the debt energetically but also chemically and physically destructive.

THE SUPERPOWER OF EMPATHY

The experience of any emotion is unique and personal. No one can fully know what it is to be you, and in the same manner, you are only capable of perceiving a small or big slice—but a slice nonetheless—of the complex multidimensionality of others. Remember, you are gifted with a valve that processes infinity into time, space, and matter. That valve also processes the experience of the interaction with others into what humans label as mind, body, and spirit.

Despite having a mind, a body, and something of another kind that transcends the previous two, humans are in the early stages of understanding and mastering what this means, much like a baby starting to gain control of their bodies and starting to crawl.

Human beings are also gifted with more than five senses. It just so happens that because five of them are more obvious and, as a human race, we can agree on a universal label, those are the ones you and I learn in school. One of the extra senses you have is called *empathy*.

Empathy is your ability to perceive the energetic signature of an emotion that either belongs to you or someone else.

Empathy does not mean that you can feel the same thing another person is feeling, even if you and someone else are feeling sadness at the same time and for the same reason. You are not inside their body, nor their mind. You are experiencing *you* all the time, and processing the outside world through your filters... all the time. Emotions are as personal as reality, and reality is the personal decoding of the outer world into each of our inner worlds.

I could write a whole book about every single one of the emotions described in "Creatures of the Deep Dark," because the experience of them is as rich as the number of humans on this planet. My intention in that section, I simply provide you with a reading of the energetic signature of the emotion, as experienced in the *collective subconscious* of the human race. It was purposefully written in a dissociative language so that you may read it and connect with it emotionally, only if there is something for you to work on at the moment. If there is, your unconscious mind will give you a sign, perhaps in the form of an emotion or a memory that causes some form of discomfort.

This book is about taking the journey into the unexplored chambers of your mind, and using the flashlight of awareness to look at ideas and beliefs that have been hidden in the dark for a while. Through this book, I am guiding you on where to point the flashlight, and helping you decode what it is that you are looking at so that you continue the journey of transforming stuck energy into energy with a purpose, and become the embodiment of energy in motion.

If "swimming in the dark" has left you feeling troubled due to a new realization, I encourage you to answer the following questions: *What would the person that loves you the most, tell you about this (that situation that is causing you a negative emotion)? What would you tell the person you love the most, if they were to share with you (that same situation that is causing a negative emotion)?*

By pushing empathy outside of yourself, and using your imagination to embody it with someone else, you will be able to obtain a beautiful learning or a precious piece of advice to continue your powerful transformation journey with self-compassion.

THE ILLUSION OF DROWNING IN A GLASS OF WATER

In reality, there is not a lot happening out there in the world around you; our planet is a gentle giant that takes its time with things. It has been around long before us, and it will continue to float in space long after we are gone.

Ninety percent of reality is happening inside your mind, and inside the minds of the 7.4 billion humans out there. There are as many realities as there are human minds. Each mind is as complex as it is imperfectly perfect, yet with all the games the mind likes to play, you and I end up feeling like we are drowning in our own games, drowning in our own separate glasses of water.

It is now time to integrate everything that you have read up until now, so that you can look at the big picture and see the world available to you beyond your glass of water. You do not need to continue swimming in there all alone, running out of air and resources. Remember what it means to be human, and understand it so that you can transcend it.

Here it is.

The 10% of your mind that functions at the conscious level is the domain of cognitive behaviors, logic, sense, creation of ideas, decisions, conscious beliefs, where you choose to continue reading this book instead of scrolling through your phone, and much more. The 90% of your mind functioning at the unconscious level is the domain of energy, emotions, values, subconscious beliefs, and also much more.

Ninety percent of the time, you get caught up in the 10% of your mind, the conscious mind, because you like to be in control of things and understand how they work and where you stand in relationship to the world around you. Not having a handle on things, generally speaking, feels unsafe to your reptilian brain, the amygdala. The ego is a part of your identity that appears somewhere between the conflicting territory of the amygdala and the prefrontal cortex. It likes to veil aspects of your awareness and keep you too caught up in your self-talk, incurring a form of self-hypnosis where you end up believing your unwarranted negative emotions and limiting decisions to be the true grossly distorted reality.

A limiting decision is any decision you have made about yourself or the world that causes pain or prevents you from growing. Pain usually is a sign to pay attention in the "now," and is a message sent from the unconscious mind via the purposeful negative emotions.

Because societal structures do not educate you nor encourage you to explore your emotional IQ, you often walk around like a starved and confused zombie, carrying heavy emotional baggage with you.

Changing and growing by choice is always an option, until it is not. Who knows how long you have been walking around numb? Having to change happens because, sooner or later, you are stripped of an aspect of your ego or a certainty you were taking for granted.

When that happens, you might experience either a warranted period of grief or an archetypical period of victimhood, being at effect, blaming others or the circumstances, and swimming in your own pain for a little too long. Sooner or later, you take charge, either because you see the light of reason or because there is no one else left to clean up your mess, and you get down to making lemonade with the lemons you have. You will certainly realize that in taking the inspired action of making lemonade, it will attract other wonderful people who like lemonade, and who have a similar story to share.

For as long as you feel human emotions, there is something to do, somewhere to go, and someone to share it with, because emotions are the energy of life. And one of the biggest secrets is that emotions serve as a compass to guide you in the path of coherence toward your deepest desires and your life's purpose.

Now that you have completed a successful initiation into the school of emotions, and the integration of new ways of looking at old stuff, let me take you on another journey of exploring some of the funniest and oddest problems humans create for themselves—from second guessing the purpose of our brains, to behaving like crabs in a bucket, or being unable to choose an ice-cream flavor and choosing to procrastinate.

I know you cannot wait to read more on that…

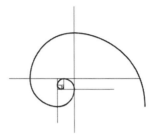

CHAPTER 8
HUMAN PROBLEMS

GOOD APPLE, BAD APPLE: JUDGING THOUGHTS

A thought is just a thought. It is a gift of the human mind to observe possibilities in the eye of imagination as part of our creative power. This is the power of sight in the invisible world, out of which humans can create things that have never existed before. When Edison envisioned the lightbulb, he might have used his imagination to know what capturing a flash of lightning to light his living room could have looked like, and then he went on to create it.

A thought by itself is of no harm to anyone. You are not activating the law of attraction by thinking it, nor are you making it *true* by simply considering it.

Human history is filled with examples of attempts to eradicate thoughts, and in some religions, certain thoughts were punished as sins.

To label a thought as positive or negative is to imply that one should or shouldn't have it at the same time one is experiencing that thought. What a discrepancy indeed! This statement also applies to emotions. It is of humans to have thoughts and emotions; it is of enlightened beings to decide upon which to act and which to let fly by.

So to imply that you should or shouldn't have certain thoughts or emotions is in itself a paradoxical curse that creates a loophole of hell between trying really hard not to have that specific thought or emotion, and then being consumed by shame or guilt for having it.

The secret to getting out of the limiting idea that you should or shouldn't have certain thoughts or emotions is to know that a thought or an emotion by itself doesn't have enough energy to manifest itself or to cause a cascade of unfortunate events. The recipe to affect your reality is incomplete, so you do not need to fear as it is lacking the energy that infuses it with life: emotion.

To observe a thought devoid of emotion, and to experience an emotion without a series of consequential thoughts, is like looking at apples hanging from an apple tree. To observe them does not make them yours, other than for the experience of acknowledging their existence.

Let's go with apples in a tree as a metaphor for how affecting your reality through the use of thought and emotion works. First of all, to deny the existence of the apple tree that is clearly in front of you would be to waste precious energy in denial. Like mentioned before, you do not need to fear looking at the tree and the apples, which represent thoughts or emotions, because looking at them does not affect your physical reality. You will not cause an accident simply by observing a rotten apple, which metaphorically stands for seeing an accident in your imagination.

To affect your reality, you would need to focus on a specific apple. And remember, since emotions are the energy of life, if you held no purposeful feelings or emotions towards that specific apple, you would not act upon your idea to grab it.

Let's say a certain apple represents your desire to start an online business selling handmade jewelry. The first step is to focus your attention and intention on that specific apple, and then take action to reach and grab that apple. Taking action can mean anything from taking a course on how to make jewelry, to hiring a website designer, to having an online business coach. Action has to be planned so that it helps you reach your desired *apple* as fast as possible, and I must add, as fun as possible!

In your life, you choose a particular apple, perhaps because of its size or because it looks shinier than the others. You wouldn't have picked the rotten apples on the ground, nor the ones on the tree that seem to be inhabited by worms, unless you had a very specific purpose for them, like throwing them at someone.

This is the power of choice. Where there is one apple, there is also the possibility of millions of others to choose from; where there is one thought, there are also the infinite possible thoughts you could choose from at any given moment in time. The power of choice is activated when you focus on the apple, or thought, you want to grab; and then you take action, no matter how big or small, which will get you in the direction of that apple.

You can ask yourself what the most nurturing thought or emotion is that you would like to reach out and grab at this moment. Which one is the juiciest, prettiest, and best-serving thought you could have right now? And just like how you would reach for an apple, you would do the same to reach and grab a thought.

Choosing healthy and nurturing thoughts is a no-brainer in theory, but how is it that in practice, we get incredibly critical about what we feed our bodies, and yet we are very irresponsible with what we choose to feed our minds? Why is it that more often than not, in our society, most people live their lives as if they are picking 10 rotten apples, leaving the good ones on the tree, and taking the bad ones back home to their family and friends, to either share them or leave them there, where they will continue to rot and mold and stink in the kitchen of their minds?

All thoughts and emotions are meant to be observed, just like the apples on a tree. Stop wronging yourself for looking at rotten apples (thoughts). The ability to discern between a rotten thought and a fruitful one is the ability to see contrast. The ability to see contrast will allow you to decide where you want to focus your attention. Once your attention is set in the right direction, take any form of action, big or small, that will get you closer to a juicy outcome.

Take one step at a time, but it all starts with choosing your apples wisely.

CRABS IN A BUCKET: WHAT HAPPENS WHEN YOU CHANGE?

It is said that to grow older is to grow wiser. But as we collectively travel the ebb and flow of life, within certain communities, we might start overindulging in detrimental behaviors such as spreading office gossip or the victim count on the newest world pandemic. And so, instead of maintaining our energy in the purposeful functions of the prefrontal cortex, we start feeding the amygdala, where the fears and limiting perceptions of the world, and of each other, grow.

Instead of growing wiser, we become like crabs in a bucket: Put one crab inside and it will find a way to get out; put several crabs inside, and they will keep pulling at each other and will remain trapped inside.

The bucket could be your home, your job, the gym, a book club, or even your chosen group of friends. The bucket is familiar territory, possibly where amygdala-fueled behaviors, and cocktails of stress hormones, thrive. Sometimes you have been in the bucket a little too long to realize that you are stuck in an endless loophole that keeps draining your energy.

What are the signs that you might be stuck inside a bucket with other crabs? And most importantly, how do you know it might be time to get out of that bucket?

Some of the signs include feeling very heavy or drained after being in a certain environment or with certain people. You might start catching yourself, more often than not, being a participant in negative conversations about the weather, another person, or problems of various natures. There seems to be no one you can turn to that has a new and fresh perspective on things; it's as if everyone suffered from the same problems as you all the time. The feeling of being in that specific environment puts you in a fight, flight, or numbing state. When faced with a new obstacle, you either become very easily overwhelmed, or you can only see option A or B, forgetting all the other letters in the alphabet.

One of the biggest signs of growing danger is when the feeling of being in this bucket overflows into all of the other areas of your life, and it drains the joy out of your heart. If you are no longer able to find peace and time for yourself and those you love, or if your health starts decaying, it is most certainly time to leave.

Several years ago, I was faced with the choice of moving up in the corporate world of personal training, or to break free as an entrepreneur. I have always been a very odd crab, and during the six years that I was working inside that particular bucket, I was usually undisturbed by the doings or "un-doings" of other crabs. My focus was 100% on the breakthroughs that my clients and I co-created, and I was always inventing new games and having a lot of fun inside that bucket—until it was not fun anymore.

The heat inside the bucket grew to a boiling point and, when that happened, the crabs inside the bucket started turning on each other. There were also other survival strategies that I watched myself and those around me execute—like fight, flight, avoid, grow numb, and play death. As I narrate this, I am very well aware that this perception of reality could have been mine and not anyone else's, but one thing was for certain: My inner world was closing in, my health was collapsing, and I had no life outside that bucket anymore.

It took a lot of courage for me to convince myself that if I left, everything was going to be okay, especially because the only thing I knew from the outer world were the stories I had heard from crabs within my bucket of people who had left and the calamities they had encountered.

The thing about staying too long inside any of these types of buckets is that either it gets very aggressive, and crabs turn to survival mode, or they eventually stop fighting and become dormant. In either case, the functions of the prefrontal cortex, where all the hope and creative energy is for being in control of your future, start shutting down and becoming dormant for months, years, or decades. To wake up a little too late is sometimes to face the pain of a chronic illness, the loss of a marriage, or the pain of regret for a wasted life.

When a crab wakes up and starts making its way up the bucket, the collective unconscious of the tribe feels threatened and might exhibit incoherent behaviors toward that individual. To the collective unconscious of those enthralled in mass hypnosis, the awakened mind might appear as delusional and even threatening.

History shows the fascinating phenomena of how some were made temporary idols by rebellious mobs, most were prosecuted and executed, and the few became famous, hundreds of years after they challenged the status quo and died. Socrates was convicted at trial, and executed by poison, in 399BC; 16th-century philosopher, Bruno Giordano, was burned at the stake; and women, accused of being witches, were burned at the stake, well up until the late 1700s. Because it is no longer legal to burn people at the stake, who knows how many more awakened minds have been silenced, and in what other ways.

You might think that this is the subject matter of movies and historical novels, but you know the stories; you have heard them at your workplace, at the gym, and at your child's school. The world is no longer led by trusted leaders either. The change will not come from high above; it is us *crabs* that need to link hands and start building up our own exit ladder.

THE CHOCOLATE OR VANILLA CURSE, COURTESY OF YOUR POWER OF CHOICE

Have you ever seen a small child caught up in the troubling decision of having to choose between two ice-cream flavors? The last time I watched a little girl being encouraged by her parents to choose either a chocolate or a vanilla ice-cream, I painfully watched her have a breakdown. Despite the loving encouragement she was receiving from her parents, the more they encouraged, the more upset she got until, unable to choose, she was taken away in tears and without any ice-cream at all.

When you feel trapped in an environment, which could be at work or even at home, your mind is a lot like a six-year-old child: distressed because you have to choose between chocolate and vanilla. And yes, what I mean is that even the simplest decisions can be incredibly overwhelming and add to the stress you are already experiencing.

One of the consequences of being trapped with other crabs in a bucket is the decay in the cognitive ability you have to solve problems. If you notice that you can only come up with two solutions to the problems in front of you, you are most certainly suffering from the *Chocolate or Vanilla Curse.* If you have been cursed, at worst, you are most certainly experiencing tunnel vision, with one way out of a problem; and at best, with two ways out: A or B; chocolate or vanilla.

At its optimum, the prefrontal cortex allows you to efficiently make decisions by easily seeing the big picture, and effortlessly thinking outside the box and coming up with multiple solutions to any given problem. Also, like you learned at the beginning of this chapter, by being able to look at all the apples on the tree. Using your creativity, which is a higher cognitive function, you might even come up with innovative solutions and ideas that have never been thought of before in your workplace or at home. This can only happen when you can calmly access all of the brain power you have; and you can easily do that when you are not stressed out or feeling frazzled.

But when the amygdala starts sucking too much energy from the smaller and older part of your brain due to stress, your world of possibilities closes in, and you start to suffer from tunnel vision, or like explained before, the *Chocolate or Vanilla Curse.*

More often than not, during the first two weeks of working with a client, they often share with me that one of their biggest problems is having to make a choice between A or B. The next thing I ask about is *how long they have been trying to make a choice.* The usual response ranges between two weeks and two months, but in some specific cases that fall into a category that need a deeper dive, the answer is two-plus years. It is obvious to me that on top of the stress my client might be experiencing due to their perceived lack of options, every moment they spend without making a decision or taking action, adds to the stress and/or the pain toll as well.

The *Chocolate or Vanilla Curse* is one of the three main reasons you and everyone else on this planet consciously or unconsciously chooses to procrastinate. Once a person manages to see the bigger picture, and his or her world opens up with a floodgate of answers, that brings another set of reasons why someone might choose to continue procrastinating.

The next chapter will take you on a deeper dive to understand why making a choice is not as simple as it looks, and bring to light two more unconscious reasons why the power to procrastinate seems like the easy way out.

THE POWER TO PROCRASTINATE

Your eyes are open, awake, aware, and alive. And now what?

Do you get out of bed, or do you hit snooze three more times? Do you answer your texts first, or do you take a pee first? Between the moment you wake up and the time you are about to start working on your day job, you have already been your own motivational coach, stylist, and cook, and have automatically forecasted your day and managed your time and energy investments. All of this happens on autopilot, and what a wonder it is indeed that by the time you consciously command yourself to start your *real job,* your mind has already been working at the executive level. By that time, you have already made between thirty and fifty decisions that have shaped who you are and also the world around you.

With so much mind power constantly at work, why is it then that some simple choices seem to put a real strain on the mind, creating a turmoil of emotions? Choices are like doors: You either open them or keep them closed, and sometimes one can stare at the door for a little too long. It is okay to take some time to make sure you are opening the right door, but procrastinating like a pro can lead to the painful realization that you are wasting your life away.

You learned that the *Chocolate or Vanilla Curse* happens as a result of stress, and it is the experience that your world is closing in where it seems like you only have two options, or two doors to choose from. Furthermore, the reason to procrastinate arises from knowing that behind door number one and door number two, there are different kinds of pain—no wonder you don't want to choose.

There are two other main reasons that you can find yourself procrastinating on making a choice, and it is of utmost importance that you bring this to the light of your awareness so that you can identify the best method to make a decision and move forward faster.

The second reason I want you to explore is "FOMO." This is the popular acronym used by today's online generation: FOMO = Fear Of Missing Out. This refers to the subconscious fear that by making a choice of a single item among many others, you end up missing out on all the other options. In this case, having too many options to choose from is the actual problem, contrary to the *Chocolate and Vanilla Curse*. The bigger the number of options from which to choose, the bigger the *fear of missing out*, and the more you procrastinate, which more often than not results in "choice paralysis."

This is the reason that successful sale strategies are often limited to two or three options at maximum. While a good salesperson still wants you to feel that you retain power of choice, they do not want you to experience "FOMO" in the face of 10 options that will make you walk away.

The third reason that I want you to be aware of, so that you can stop procrastinating, is the fear to take responsibility for a choice. To make a choice is indeed to take ownership of your power to affect your reality, and sometimes that of those around you. There is a part of you that is highly sensitive to the personal and collective impact of your choices. To that part, every choice you make is like throwing a pebble into a pond, which causes a ripple effect on the water. Procrastinating on making a choice might have to do with the unconscious fear you have of such a ripple effect, especially when there are others involved.

Be watchful of the need to procrastinate as an unconscious strategy to divert responsibility, expecting someone else to make a choice for you, or waiting for the situation to resolve on its own. If you do that, you are like a boat in the middle of the sea, at the mercy of the wind—who knows where you will end up?—and the last thing you want is a storm to sink your ship.

Shining the light on the reasons you procrastinate is mindful practice as powerful as meditation itself. Once you can pinpoint the reason you are procrastinating, it is more likely that you can get unstuck and start moving in the direction you want to go. As you become more aware of your personal power, staying stuck out of lack of options cannot be an option anymore.

You now have brought to your conscious awareness three normally unconscious reasons for why you might be procrastinating, and whether the solution is increasing the options for the *Chocolate or Vanilla Curse*, or reducing the options for FOMO, the ultimate solution is to make a choice and take a small action, any small action, and the sooner the better.

The next time you make a powerful choice, I want you to pay attention to the relief and space you feel inside, and remember that.

This will encourage you to continue choosing powerfully and to keep building your *choice muscle*. Procrastination is only a power if you consciously choose to procrastinate and can deal with the consequences of your choice.

I am constantly adding resources on my website to assist you in traveling into the unexplored territories of the unconscious mind, and learning more about your super powers. Take a look at the resources I provide for working out your power to choose, and head over to the next section to learn more about why humans are not capable of living in paradise.

DESTRUCTIVE ABUNDANCE AND OUR DEMISE FROM PARADISE

Abundance and destruction are not words you would normally hear in the same sentence, let alone married together in a title. You might wonder how abundance could be destructive. I am sure that all of us could always use a little more time, a little more money, a little more charisma—a little more of something—and then our lives would be so much better. And most certainly, you and I wouldn't say no to a winning lottery ticket. Winning the lottery is the abundance cliché of our times. But there is a big difference between a little bit more and having it all.

Humankind has been warned to slow down and learn what it takes to handle abundance. In this section, you will learn of three different warnings encoded in our collective reality, and the lessons that you as an individual must learn in order to get what you want—whether its money, health, love, freedom, or anything else you have been wishing for.

The Bible contains the first warning. Adam and Eve had it all and lived without lack in paradise... and then the whole soap opera of the snake and the apple happened, and they were kicked out. You will find that across the globe, in many religious and spiritual scriptures, both ancient and recent, a similar story is contained about how humankind is experiencing the separation from an *absolute nurturing wholeness*. Some teachings hint, and some are very clear that this separation is being experienced out of choice; for example, the choice Adam and Eve made to eat the apple even though they were told not to do so. And all religious and spiritual teachings describe a way of being that will allow a person to return back to Source and the bliss of this archetypical paradise. Various teachings do seem to have a different way of saying the same thing, and you will be able to see that once you get past the surface embellishments of the narrative.

Paradise sounds really nice in theory, and you might believe it exists, or you might not. And if it does, the requirements to enter sound like a lot of work, and the small print says that you have to die in order to enter. No one wants to think about going through that door now. But wait; you actually do not need to go through all of that to experience paradise, and you might have experienced paradise on Earth already!

If you think about it, all-inclusive vacations are mini versions of paradise. At least they are at first sight. Upon further investigation, they are a lot more like a test.

If you think back to a time when you had been to one, or heard from someone you know who went to one, you are very well aware that not many people pass the *Paradise Test*. Whether its food, alcohol, sex, drugs, parties, sun, or a combination of these items, what starts like paradise ends in sins worthy of any of the seven hells from Dante Alighieri's *Divine Comedy*.

Energy in Motion

The lesson here is to take paradise in small increments, lest you end up in hell. This is the second warning. Throughout your life, you have had and will continue to have mini *Paradise Tests*. Whether it is a long vacation, a period of extraordinary energy and motivation, or a work raise or bonus, there are many forms in which you will experience more money, time, and energy. What you do at that time, and how you use those resources, will give you insightful information on your readiness to enter *paradise*.

The third warning comes from *nature,* and it has been encrypted in our genetic code. You and I are a part of nature, whether we acknowledge it or not.

Observing nature as a frame of reference for what is normal, natural, and balanced can be of great help in looking for answers. When it comes to abundance, would any wild animal take more than what it can chew? Does any tree absorb more water than what it can process? Certainly not. An overfed wild animal will either be eaten or be unable to chase new prey. Its survival is compromised either way. An overwatered tree will rot and die. But unlike human beings, none of these living entities have a consciousness that is always striving for more. To be awake, aware, and alive as a human, can be both a blessing and a curse. What a curse it is to live alone in an empty mansion, to eat out of boredom, and to have more time on our hands than what we can handle—sarcasm intended—and yet for some of us, myself included, this has been a personal source of suffering. Maybe leaving paradise was not such a bad idea after all, and maybe Earth is the perfect school to learn how to earn back the trust we need in order to know that we can handle absolute abundance.

Humans have walked the face of the Earth for several million years now. From the time our ancestors were hunters and gatherers, up until the early 1800s, not a lot had changed. For most humans, every hour of the day was accounted for and needed to count toward food and shelter. The Industrial Revolution saw the birth of machinery that opened up the gateway for mass production and mass consumption. Between 1900 and 2020, the population grew from under 2 billion to an estimate of 8 billion humans on this same planet. This means that in just 100 years the human population quadrupled, while prior to that it took more than a million years for humans to add up to just 1 million! This is an incredibly shocking revelation with deep rooted implications.

Just to open up the conversation to one of many implications, the genetic material that has shaped us as a species certainly has not had the time to catch up with the level of abundance we are capable of manifesting, and that is why you cannot have what you want. If the Universe, or God, or luck, or nature, were to hand you what you wanted, that would be similar to you handing the keys of a Mercedes to a 15-year-old, expecting him or her to behave responsibly with it. We have been warned, and we have been tested, as you now have learned, and possibly have failed many times. We are in fact currently failing at how we handle our planet's resources, at a catastrophic rate.

And yet epigenetics, the study of gene alteration through human consciousness, is here to tell you how you can alter your genes now, and purposefully adapt to change and match up to the infinite possibilities you can envision in your mind's eye, whatever they are. Not only that, within 50 years, if we make the necessary changes we could also replenish the resources of our planet by 1/3. I am of that mind too, and that is why I have written this book as a doorway for you to start making consciousness of small aspects of your personal power and the impact of it on a larger scale. But I will reserve the bigger picture for my next two books.

Energy in Motion

If you do not yet have the health, wealth, love, happiness, house, and other things that you want, it is because you are being called to change in order to have it. The question you must ask yourself is: *Who do you (I) need to become in order to have it?*

Check out the exercise on my website, on "Destructive Abundance," to continue to explore your return to paradise.

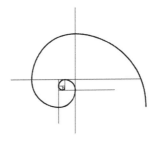

CHAPTER 9
THE BLUEPRINT TO HIGHER CONSCIOUSNESS

THE GOLDEN RATIO AND THE GOD OF MATH

Archetype is a term attributed to Jungian theory, and it refers to a metaphorical blueprint capable of capturing a universal occurrence; or in other words, a way of being that transcends age groups, cultures, and historical times. Take, for example, The Hero's Journey. This blueprint outlines the story of a character, or hero in question, who leaves his certainties behind, undertakes a journey of discovery with its set of complications and monsters, overcomes obstacles, wins a victory or two, and comes back changed.

Does this story sound familiar? This is the story told in *Energy in Motion*. It starts with a *certainty* as the opening act, followed by *change,* which triggers a contrast or conflict out of which emotional disruption arises. A journey of self-discovery is taken, either through avoidance or purposeful action, in order to reach another chapter of blissful growth and peaceful certainty. And then it starts all over again.

This is also the story of your life, my life, and the rest of humankind. Life can be described as one big journey composed of many smaller quests, or many small quests that sum up to the adventure of a lifetime.

The Hero's Journey, as an archetypical blueprint, proves to be an invaluable tool for introspection. Whether you think of yourself as a hero or villain, you certainly are the main character in the story. This is your story and your search for meaning. Humans are, by nature, *meaning-making machines*, who get super excited to find out that we are not alone and misunderstood, despite the contrasting need to feel unique and special.

Energy in Motion

You can obtain a diagram of the Hero's Journey on my site. The "Hero's Journey" was a term popularized by Joseph Campbell's work in the mid-1900s, although archetypical storytelling dates back to over 20,000 years ago, when humans started recording aspects of their lives in cave paintings.

Due to the subjective nature of archetypes as metaphorical maps, they can be quite controversial. However, an archetype transcends its subjective nature when it encounters mathematics. Math is the god of this Universe, due to the simple collective agreement that anything that can be proven with a mathematical formula will be accepted as truth. In other words, when a subjective perception of reality, in this case an archetype, can be captured by a mathematical formula, it grounds it as universally true for all. Can you argue that $1+1 = 2$? I am sure there are some awakened minds that can argue the truth of that, but this is a subject that belongs in another of my books.

Here is the fascinating thing about change: From the Big Bang theory to the arrangement of the petals in a rose, from the position of our solar system to the ratio and positioning of your eyes in relationship to your nose, there is a mathematical code that repeats itself over and over and over again. It is called the *Golden Ratio*.

The Golden Ratio proves, with numbers and science, that we live in an organized and harmonic Universe, in continuous expansion. From the micro-universe of cells to the macro-cosmos, from the impersonal world of elements to the personal experience of life, the Golden Ratio is the map that holds the key to understanding why history repeats itself, both personally and at world scale, and why breakdowns and breakthroughs lead the way for a Universe in constant expansion, and more importantly how to navigate through a world in constant change.

But none of this knowledge matters if a person goes through life without learning how to navigate it. The following section will assist you in creating a link between the macro map of the Golden Ratio and the micro scale of your personal life. It will also provide a fresh perspective on the roller coaster of life, which can help free your mind.

But before you head there, go to EnergyinMotionBook.com, and in the Resource section, have a look at the Mind Maps. They will help you put into perspective the information contained in this chapter.

HIGHS, LOWS, AND FLOWS

Describing life as a roller coaster seems to be the preferred method to describe the highs and lows of the human experience. Similar to the Golden Ratio, the Roller Coaster is a metaphorical map that describes the linear experience of traveling through life: The ups symbolize the emotions on the positive side of the scale, and the downs symbolize those on the low side of the scale; the climbs represent the strenuous, slow, and sometimes boring periods of hard work, while the downward slopes represent the scary and exhilarating times of adventure, change, and enjoying the fruits of hard labor.

But have you noticed that there are people out there that seem to defy the law of the roller coaster? These individuals seem to effortlessly float along in life while still getting all the benefits of the ride, but without having to experience the cursed burnout. To the normal eye, they appear as happy-go-lucky, unpredictable, phony, or too good to be true. Upon further investigation, you might notice that they also possess other traits. They are creative, energetic, and disruptive, with an uncanny ability to shapeshift as required.

Perhaps one of the reasons why these unique individuals seem to live in a different reality is because, knowingly or unknowingly, their mental maps of life are different than those of the status quo. Remember that the status quo is, by default, trapped inside a box as you learned in the section *Crabs in a Bucket: What Happens When You Change?*, and has a pattern of accepting that which fits the norm, and wronging that which doesn't.

It doesn't matter where your current mental map has taken you in life; the state of ease and effortless flow is accessible to you as well. I know it, and even if you don't, in this world, it is enough for one person to know it and believe it, even if that person is not you. So, in the meantime, let me hold that belief for you while you catch up to your full potential.

While most people seem to have a preference for a linear way of mapping time, like *The Roller Coaster Map*, this personal preference has its set of limitations. To accept the Roller Coaster as the archetypical map to live your life, is also to accept the limiting decisions that come with it.

Let me explain this further. When you agree that life is like a roller coaster, without taking the time to learn the unconscious implications of complying with that map, it is a lot like signing a contract without reading the fine print. Some of the limiting decisions that might come with this map include, but are not limited to, experiencing a low after a high, and having to exert a lot of energy or effort in climbing up that slope, only for brief peak experiences. Suffering from the crabs in a bucket syndrome, whether you are the crab trying to get out, or unknowingly the one pulling someone down, is also a limiting decision that arises out of feeling stuck in a low, within the linear perception of time, within *The Roller Coaster Map*.

In the world of bodybuilding, *The Roller Coaster* Map is quite popular. The "post-show blues" and weight gain are regarded as the norm; however, there are individuals who cracked the code on how to manage their emotions, and actually fall outside the behavioral norm of weight gain and post-show struggles. As a result, they trigger the crabs in a bucket syndrome in those stuck in the norm, and get highly criticized for being different. To observe this collective behavior is quite the ride in itself. To read more stories that inspired *Energy in Motion,* go to the blog section on my website.

Here is the reason why you should always aim for a better mind map.

Your mind map is a set of rules you have, to process and make sense of the world around you. Your mind map is like the bus driver in a bus full of beliefs and behaviors; so instead of trying to change the passengers one at a time, which can take a lot of time, let's change the bus driver and head in a different direction right away.

Aim right now for a higher mind map than that of the Roller Coaster.

Expand your mind to include the Golden Ratio as a new mind map to navigate your life's adventures and misadventures. Its circular nature allows for the acknowledgement of the ups and downs but in the context of growing within flow.

Flow is a state of effortless motion, much like how the Tao describes the experience of how water encounters a rock and flows effortlessly around it. While someone in a state of flow is very

Energy in Motion

capable of experiencing the full spectrum of emotions, from rage to joy, and depression to exhilaration, the experience does not put them in a state of victimhood. While remaining at cause, someone in a state of flow is capable of becoming the observer, standing on the sidelines, and going with the flow when no action is needed, as well as powerfully moving mountains when they are called into action.

There are other amazing benefits to learning how to maintain a state of flow.

To the person in flow, life appears easy and effortless. This person experiences a continuous influx of energy and a childlike curiosity and desire to continue exploring and experiencing life. The feeling of resting can be achieved simply by changing activities or context. Tunnel vision is no longer experienced and, instead, the senses seem to open and take in a world of possibilities. Other senses beyond the five senses kick in, and the person experiences a natural connection with everyone and everything around them. There is an integration of intellect, emotion, and information, and experiences appear as multilayered or as if holding multiple meanings. The experience of time and space changes.

You might have tapped into a state of flow at some moment in your life, which possibly was mistaken for a high in *The Roller Coaster Map* because you weren't aware that this was a new level of awareness.

Remember, you don't know what you don't know, until someone points it out. But you do not need to wrong yourself. Know that a *Roller Coaster Map* is not a mapping error either; it is in fact a developmental step in the early stages of a consciousness waking up to being at cause and acknowledging change. And in order for things to change, there is a natural ebb and flow of opposite forces, both of which must exist in order for you to keep growing. Learn more about the balance of these forces in the next section.

BREAKDOWNS AND BREAKTHROUGHS

The map is not the territory, but it is certainly reassuring to know one is not lost by having a reference that tells us where we are.

As you have learned, there are various blueprints or archetypical maps that you can use to gain a broader understanding of what stage you find yourself at, with the purpose of navigating negative emotions, limiting decisions, obtaining learnings, and expanding or creating personal boundaries.

Some of the maps I have mentioned are the Hero's Journey, the Roller Coaster, and the Golden Ratio. The Golden Ratio can also be thought of as the map of maps. It is universal and all-encompassing in nature, and most maps are but pieces of the puzzle within it. The Golden Ratio is not a unidimensional map either, but my observations on multidimensionality are part of a latter book in the *Energy in Motion* series.

The collective human consciousness currently has a preference for a two-dimensional, horizontal, and linear model of storing, studying, and understanding the passage of time. The Roller Coaster map arises out of this linear experience of time.

There is a moment in our lives before we reach adulthood, where we erroneously believe that reaching adulthood is about gaining a static sense of certainty and fulfillment; but in fact, part of the process of reaching adulthood is acknowledging that ups and downs are part of the cycle of life, and more so of the adult life.

Energy in Motion

As our consciousness grows, and our vocabulary to describe the world of the mind becomes more sophisticated, ups and downs, happy and sad, eventually evolve into something more colorful, like breakthroughs and breakdowns, exhilaration and anguish. Words create realities, and the more expansive our vocabulary, the more expansive our reality becomes.

A breakdown is defined in most modern dictionaries as a physical failure to function, a mechanical disruption, or a loss of mental health.

A breakdown, at its lowest point, is often called "the dark night of the soul." One of my favorite depictions of this experience is the swamp scene from the movie *The NeverEnding Story*, where the hero is stuck in mud up to his chest and is in danger of sinking deeper after having experienced a profound personal loss.

All of these frames of reference most certainly tell us to point all efforts in trying to avoid a breakdown at any cost.

But the word "breakdown" in itself simply implies an experience of falling apart or undoing of something, without any further connotation. It is us—the human *meaning-making machines*—that make all the assumptions that follow with a devastating story of emotional turmoil.

The word "breakdown" could not exist without its opposing force, which is a "breakthrough." New ideas and new houses can be built upon old structures; however, if the old structure is rotten and no longer serves a purpose, the new idea or the new house will rot as well. A breakdown implies a clean slate, on which a solid new idea, foundation, or house can be built, literally and metaphorically speaking.

THE DARK NIGHT OF THE SOUL

A breakdown is characterized by a shift in consciousness to the unexplored territories of your mind, which usually give rise to emotions on the dark side of the emotional spectrum. The feeling of tapping into inactive sections and dormant neurons of your mind is quite uncomfortable at its best, and highly volatile at its worst.

Maybe the scene from the movie, where the hero is trying to walk his way through chest high mud, is very similar to the feeling of awakening. Whether it's the physical experience of activating dormant grey matter in the brain, or shining a light on dark aspects of the mind, there is sure to be an upheaval and rebellion of sorts.

Most people describe facing negative emotions such as confusion, feeling alone, disconnected, lethargic, and helplessly sinking, with the expectation to reach rock bottom before starting to feel any better. There is also a hidden hope that someone can come and save them from this swamp, or that the circumstances will magically change to favor them. This, unfortunately, gives away personal power to something or someone else, leaving a person at the effect side of things, instead of at cause.

The process gets more strenuous when a person is constantly wronging themselves for feeling this way, or fighting with all their might and effort against the only thing they are not in control of: the will of others.

There is a defining moment during the battle at the swamp, where someone who lacks the awareness of context, the willingness to change, or the resources needed to do so, could possibly lose the fight and sink down into the "dark night of the soul."

Sinking down into the swamp is a very real experience, but there is more to it than just a horrible and chaotic breakdown. Sinking down emotionally also signals the unconscious mind to go into a dormant and less demanding state, because whatever was happening was too much for the person's conscious mind to handle. The unconscious mind has the capability to store the lesson for future use, once a hero has regained their strength.

Whether the hero in question sinks down or makes it through the swamp, it is not a matter of giving up but more a matter of surrendering, much like the water opens way for the rock so that it can continue its flow. Again, whether the end result is up or down, nothing cuts the flow faster than a person's inability to let go of past aspects of themselves.

Undeniably, the circumstance a person finds themselves in requires change, and change often calls for a new version of the self. Getting stuck and staying stuck could be a result of lack of knowledge or resources, but it could also be a stubborn choice. When someone is required to break the habit of being themselves in order to overcome the swamp, things can get really scary—not just for the ego, but for the broken aspects of the ego that someone has worked so hard at building, like the victim story or the self-sabotaging character in a play.

COVID-19 AND THE BREAKDOWN OF THE SELF

Normally, a breakdown happens sporadically and in an isolated manner to individuals or social groups. Going at it alone can be freakishly troubling, as well as going at it collectively at a world scale level such as the quarantine period of COVID-19. During this time, a lot of people got stripped from the personas they had worked so hard at building, as businesses, jobs, careers, and routines went out the window in a matter of weeks. We were required to adapt or reinvent ourselves to move on. How successful do you think you were during this period? How you personally define "success" will play a big role in how you answer this question.

Some of the differences between someone capable of moving forward, versus someone who felt stuck, came down to being comfortable in breaking the habit of being defined by their job, their income, or their routine, and letting go of personality attachments of the past, flowing through negative emotions and limiting decisions that came up in stages, and navigating the unexpected, week after week after week.

Personality attachments of the past, or ego attachments, can be anything from people, to places, to things, to behaviors, beliefs, and emotions, and so many other unsuspected occurrences. The inability to let go of mental and physical aspects of your past self when required is more often than not the source of fear and pain. That might have become very obvious to a lot of people in the months following the announcement of a world pandemic.

In this book, you have read about underlying factors that can impact a person at the unconscious level, causing further fear and pain and inability to move forward. But what is truly puzzling is when someone's physical or mental health is in jeopardy, and they continue to choose to experience pain, especially if they have been presented a clear way out.

During quarantine, there were no shortages of free workouts, free coaching programs, and free soul-searching modalities being offered to people to stay grounded, focused, and ease some of the fear and anxiety they could have been experiencing. A small percentage of the population took advantage of it, but most didn't.

Energy in Motion

In a normal circumstance where someone was offered a solution to their pain and chose not to take it—for example, the perfect health program—I couldn't understand why someone would do that to themselves, even after I did that to myself for three years. It took me a lot more time to discover a simple equation that explains it.

Here it is: *When the pain of staying the same is tolerable or less painful than the need to change, the person will remain stuck or in pain, no matter how much they are suffering.*

In the abnormal case of COVID-19, and after writing *Energy in Motion*, I could see the obvious fight, flight, and amygdala responses that would have most of us frazzled, foggy, and unable to grasp what was happening, nevertheless a course of action, myself included.

The fear of the unknown is primal and real, and breaking the habit of being oneself and reinventing the circumstances requires a person to step into new, wild, and untamed territory, and take creative responsibility for that new space. To most, this is like staring into the face of darkness or walking through mud. During COVID-19, it was like trying to make sense of everything that was happening while standing on your head.

The choice to strip oneself from the past can come internally and out of choice, or externally without having a say in it. When the stripping of the past comes from external circumstances, much like it happened to those who lost their jobs due to the pandemic, the result is either oddly liberating or freakishly paralyzing. A person might even experience grief, because grief is a normal emotion experienced by an individual who perceives that there has been an incomprehensible or confusing loss in their life.

Someone in liberation mode might see that not having to commute for two hours, to work at an office for nine hours, all of a sudden means they have 11 hours of freedom a day to finally take care of their physical and mental health. These people, all of a sudden, find themselves enjoying spending time with their families, taking on all sorts of art projects, and even learning how to play guitar. This is a great time to know themselves and discover what they really want in their heart of hearts.

On the opposite end, someone in paralysis mode might now feel that they don't know who they are. Their life was defined by what they did at their jobs, for decades, and now there are 11 scary hours in the day, of emptiness and silence, or with a lot of personal demons waiting to be heard.

These are just examples of subconscious conversations that might be going on in the background as we collectively navigate the world changes that COVID-19 has brought upon us, and as we enter into new territory in the months and even years to come.

CONSCIOUSNESS EXPANDS IN BREAKDOWNS

Despite what you now know about breakdowns or undoings, you might dislike and even reject the thought that you have to go through them in order to reach new heights. You also might have the erroneous belief that the goal is to reach a certain level of consciousness or awakening, where you will no longer experience a breakdown.

I have coached numerous clients through this misunderstanding. They kept wronging themselves because they had invested lot of mindful time, energy, and money in clearing unwarranted emotions and decisions that were holding them back from living life powerfully, yet they were still encountering breakdowns. I am sharing this with you because I would like you to learn from the experience of others—something that might save you a lot of time and heartache if you were to try to figure it out on your own.

First, I helped them understand the unconscious mind map they were currently using to absorb and define their life's experiences. Some were using the Roller Coaster mapping system, and others had some fascinating unique maps of their own. Then we proceeded to incorporate their map within the Golden Ratio, and understand what part of the journey they currently found themselves in.

Some of my clients had a tremendous emotional release from simply understanding this logic, and some others needed a bit more in-depth exploration to get there, but the change was so obvious that if you were there, you would have seen the burden that was that lifted from their shoulders.

In a nutshell, what I want you to know is that breakdowns, or undoings as I like to call them, are the perfect soil for growth. They are meant to happen throughout our human lives as they follow the natural ratio for the awakening of human consciousness. Undoings eventually reach bigger and bigger loops within the Golden Ratio and, in fact, they can get incredibly educational and even exciting.

When your consciousness expands and reaches a bigger loop, you usually have the capacity to change out of choice and can clearly see the path; versus having a consciousness on a smaller loop, where you feel stuck, lack awareness or resources, and wrong yourself for experiencing negative emotions, instead of using them as fuel for growth.

At higher loops and levels of awareness, senses like gut feelings, intuition, and even what some label as common sense, are well calibrated to lead a person in redirecting their course to avoid a crash trajectory. Every day, life triggers and negative emotions hold invaluable information for the person to grow, and a person in a higher loop can see that. For example, I love my husband so much, and yet he still triggers the hell out of me. No one else can trigger me like he does, and despite the fact that I might explode in anger and unintentionally hurt him with my words, and then run to my room like a little girl to hide and cry, every day I am thankful that he shows me aspects of my personality that still need refining, and areas of love and compassion where I still need to grow.

It might take me at least couple of hours to come down from our room, say I am sorry, and then tell him what I learned about myself, all the while feeling as uncomfortable and sticky as if I had dumped a jar of honey on my head, but I eventually do it. It is quite liberating, and the breakdowns keep appearing, yet spreading themselves farther and farther apart now, just like the loops in the Golden Ratio.

Here is another example that you might find practical and relatable. You have certainly grown in awareness of the use of money in your life. You might now have a financial advisor, which would metaphorically function as your money coach, or your money shaman. So, if your financial advisor is predicting a market crash, unless you have a supernatural sense of intuition, or practice mediumship, it would be of common sense to listen to their advice and take action accordingly to avoid the pain of financial loss.

Another great example is when someone comes to the realization that they have been trying to lose weight on their own for 10 years, and they finally hire an expert in the field of nutrition and training, and find they reach their goal within a year!

These examples will also allow me to describe another great thing about having an undoing when you find yourself at a higher level of consciousness. Persons who have entered the higher loops have usually cleaned up the limiting decision that they have to go at it alone, and you will always find them surrounded by a fantastic network of uplifting individuals, in the form of coaches, communities, friends, family, and other types of human resources. The truth is that absolutely everyone is surrounded by similar resources, but without the clearing of that old limiting decision that they have to do everything on their own, they won't be able to see those resources.

The difference is personal and perceptual, but a person also needs to grow into that awareness of not having to do everything by themselves, and cannot be forced into it. Also, you do not need to be wronged by it; it is a normal stage in the process of awakening, to suffer the contrast created by the illusion that we are alone or that we have to go at it alone.

A person, a human consciousness, has the capacity to foresee the need for change, and change out of choice and not out of pain. The truth is that when life is going as planned—marriage, children, work, workouts, vacations, etc.—and everyone is happy, a person is busy enjoying all of that, and there is neither the need nor the chance to audit one's life.

One of the best things about a breakdown is that the consciousness gets shifted into the unexplored territory of the unconscious mind, and gets the chance to look at the gremlins that live there, with a flashlight. It is in that altered state of the norm of the consciousness—a breakdown—that one will speak, act, and think in ways uncommon to their habitual self. It is here that one gets to ask the tough questions and also swim in negative emotions, which the person was not allowing themselves to do when everything was going as planned. In this altered state, one also very easily breaks the habit of being themselves, even if that means behaving like a misunderstood child. To someone who prides themselves in exhibiting enormous control, a breakdown is a powerful step toward *undoing*, and testing a new way of being and growth.

A person coming out of a state of breakdown might bring with them new ideas and new ways of thinking that will be the source of much joy and wealth in the upcoming years. This is precisely the goal of having a breakdown, much like how the map of "the Hero's Journey" shows that the hero in question undertakes a quest to come back from dark roads to a better self or a better world.

I entered my last undoing six months prior to the quarantine period of COVID-19. A lot of the answers I brought back from my last "undoing," were the golden nuggets that transformed my quarantine period into one of the most fascinating times of my life. For stories, visit the blog section on my website.

Nature answers to the same code for breakdowns and breakthroughs than we do, but it does not need to call it anything. It is us humans that find labels useful and satisfying in describing aspects of our consciousness and our realities. Water, earth, wind, and fire are in constant motion, and work at undoing and reshaping the planet as needed.

In the wealth of wisdom that the Universe provides for us, you can observe that breakdowns and breakthroughs in nature happen through periods of expansion and contraction, life and death. It is as if the macro-cosmos breathes the same way as living organisms do. The Universe is in continuous expansion, breathing in two times more than it breathes out, and so it also follows the Golden Ratio.

What is the label or labels that can serve you best and describe your journey through life? What are the labels that you would like to change or continue using? The purpose of my book is to continue providing you with deeper insights so that you can integrate these concepts into your life in a way that best serves you.

From ups and downs, to breakdowns and breakthroughs, to undoing and reshaping, to expansion and contraction, find the labels that you like best because they open up your mind, and start incorporating them into your vocabulary as of today. Keep your senses open to observe the difference that this makes for you, and please be sure to share some of your stories and testimonials through the contact form on my website.

I want to hear from you.

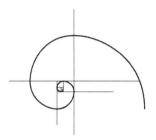

CHAPTER 10
HOW TO UNLEASH YOUR MIND

THE RESPONSIBILITY OF HUMAN CONSCIOUSNESS

Not everything that is alive has a consciousness capable of pondering upon the significance of being alive. Somewhere along the timeline of the sapiens, we sprouted the superpower to be self-aware and, in doing so, we are invariably forced to experience the consequences of the meaning, or lack of meaning, that we give to living. We are either thriving and growing in consciousness, or cursed to suffer under our own reality prisons. And whether we see it or not, we remain connected to the Universe, and who we chose to be or not to be has repercussions that will reverberate through the fabric of time and space.

Whether it is the 24 hours of a mayfly, the 82 years of a human being, or the 4,862-year- old tree, Prometheus, that found the end of its life in 1964, the fact is that any amount of life happens in the space between 2 eternities. And so there is a question worth asking: Out of all the possible times to exist, why you, why me, why here, and why now? We could have been awake, aware, and alive in the Middle Ages, or even 300 years into the future; but instead, we find ourselves intersecting in this bleep of space and time. There must be a very important reason, one that perhaps we have chosen to forget so that we can experience the exhilaration of finding ourselves again.

By thinking of ourselves as a consciousness in a vessel navigating through the sea of life, we can discuss the concept of voyaging. Just like jumping into a car as travelers, we are playing the game of getting from point A to point B, creating the illusion of separation, and experiencing the dramatization of all that we can possibly encounter in the in-between.

Perhaps it is not the journey itself, or actually getting what we want, but instead that the whole game is about who we become while we play at getting somewhere. I had to become a different person from who I have been for the past 35 years so that I could write this book, and even though the past 35 years contributed to the creation of it, the person I was one year ago could not have shared a book with the world.

Being human means that you have a responsibility to listen to the whispers of your consciousness. For you, getting your dream job, hitting your goal weight, or meeting the person that lights up your soul, has to do with the potential inside of you to be different than you are today, and with the potential to shape the physical world around you. You and only you have the power to actualize these realities and transform the world. Your desires and wishes are given to you along with the means to realize them by passing certain tests. Remember, it is not necessarily about the end goal, but who you become as you take on a hero's journey to get there.

If you are ready to learn about these tests, head over to the next section, where you can find out if you currently find yourself in front of one of the them.

THE THREE TESTS OF A HERO

Life is a collection of journeys, in the same way that a crustacean does not only change shells once or twice in its lifetime, but continues to grow for as long as it can. The changing of shells is the period in which such creatures are at their most tender and vulnerable selves. Why would they want to seek growth at the risk of being eaten by all sorts of sea predators?

It's because, by being part of this Universe, its microcosmic life mimics that of the macro-cosmos, proving that whether it is at a personal scale or at a universal scale, we all seem to follow the same call to grow, and the same map that leads in that direction, even though following the call might mean leaving safety behind.

But a person is not a crustacean, and is not bound to the rules of the Universe. In fact, despite the evidence I have given you in earlier sections about how the laws of nature apply to us, humans very much fight these rules and deny them, sometimes proving that our stubborn selves are actually so powerful, to the point of completely reshaping the very own fabric of reality. Whether in victim mode or in creator mode, we are the main characters in our own stories, and we are the creators of our own reality.

I want you to imagine that every expansion in the loops of the Golden Ratio symbolize an expanded version of a life experience or of a lesson you learned. Below, I will show you two different ways in which this map can be used.

The Age Group Map – A life Experience

Imagine that the first loop symbolizes your childhood years, where you depended on the adults around you for growth and nurturement; the second loop corresponds to your teenage years, where you experienced aggressive physical transformations and tested different personalities until you found yourself; and the third loop represents your early adult years, where all your energy is focused on finding your place in the world and what you are here to do (i.e. your job, your spouse, your place of residence).

The Personal Learnings Map – A Lesson Learned

Take the first loop as a representation of a major lesson you learned in your life, about the difference between your ego and your higher self. Some examples to choose from can be leadership, relationships, business, and love. I am going to use love to illustrate this example. The first loop could represent the first time you ever fell in love with someone and dropped your ego for that person, maybe doing things you would never do in your sane mind. The second loop could represent when you got your heart broken by this person, and the lesson in self- compassion you had to learn in order to stop beating yourself up for your mistakes. The third loop is a lesson in letting go of that relationship and finally moving on. Notice how the three loops are about the same lesson: love.

After reading the examples of the two maps above, choose one that you would like to work with, or map your own three-step lesson with a common theme before you read about the three tests.

These tests are the same in every level, yet they take different costumes every time. These three tests, or gates, are the ones you will encounter in your journey in navigating change or toward fulfilling a desire, and you must face them in order to move to higher loops of consciousness.

Let's see what they are.

Test 1: Fear

After centuries of being ruled by the amygdala, which if you remember from Chapter 2 is in charge of our survival, it is quite natural to experience the primal emotion of fear in the face of change. The real test is what a person chooses to do with that fear they experience in the face of change, and the capacity to see past that fear and discover it is a real or imagined fear.

In the Age Group Map, lesson one, the fear might be present in the realization that childhood has been left behind, and in lesson three, as the realization that you must now make sense of the adult world.

In the Personal Learnings Map, lesson two, a person might feel fear of not knowing how to love themselves; and in lesson three, the fear of putting themselves out there to date again.

Test 2: Knowledge

Despite reassuring ourselves with all our might that what we want is the truth, humans put up a big fight when being shown what "the light" is and means. Plato, the Greek philosopher, has a fantastic scripture that shows how the fear of knowledge is experienced by the human race, in the allegory of the cave, written in his work, *The Republic,* around 380 BC. On the other hand, humanity has a historical record of crucifying, ostracizing, and silencing those individuals who dared to bring new discoveries to the light.

I am going to clarify this example for you. What did you feel as a kid the day that you learned where Christmas gifts really came from? Instead of loving your parents more for the truly magical efforts and nerve curling lengths they went to, to keep the magic going, you probably cried and got angry at them in having learned the truth. At least that's what I did.

An adult who learns a truth behaves a lot similar, usually because if such truth is truly of value, it causes a breakdown in an aspect of the self-made reality. But remember, a *breakdown* usually comes before a *breakthrough*.

Test 3: Your Mirror Self

The third test is the most difficult to face; not because it's scary, but because it's veiled by the ego. The ego is not a bad thing; it is part of the construct of who we are, the part of us that makes us the main character in the story. When the ego is out of balance, it likes to make us believe that our story is the only story, and so we end up behaving like spoiled brats, thinking we are being righteous when in truth we are being narrow minded.

The mirror self-test that arises out of the ego has to do with projecting personal traits onto others. When there are people around you in your family, your job, or your community that trigger the hell out of you, that is the perfect opportunity to observe the third test at play. You wouldn't be able to perceive in others that which you do not have inside yourself. For example, I think of myself as a very weird, creative person, and sometimes I prefer not to engage with people who I perceive as "weird." When I asked my husband if he thought that such a person was weird, he said, "Not at all; the weird one is you." In introspection I learned that I was projecting the discomfort I have with myself for being weird, onto another person.

On my website, you will find a complete analysis of The Age Group Map and the Personal Learnings Map, to expand in the purpose of this chapter.

Throughout this book, you have already embarked on a personal learnings journey, where you became more aware of the spark of life contained within you, and the miracle that is in and of itself. You also learned about emotions as a communication system with your unconscious mind, and as fuel for action and transformation. You have also started to understand the valuable opportunities for growth contained within negative emotions, and that there is quite a bit of work to do when it comes to understanding the decisions you have made in the past about yourself and the world, especially if you are feeling stuck.

By unleashing your mind and allowing yourself to learn new ways of looking at the world, you can start changing your reality by changing the way you think, speak, and ultimately take action in the direction you want your life to go. But there is one more piece you will need in order to complete the puzzle contained within *Energy in Motion*. I have to tell you about another map that you carry inside your soul, another resource to continue undoing the illusion that is keeping you stuck.

YOUR SOUL MAP

The why of all whys is perhaps, "Why am I here?" and the where of all wheres is, "Where did I come from?" and "Where am I going?"

Life is indeed a collection of adventures or quests that sum up to the adventure of a lifetime. Finding purpose for the time we have allotted to be here, to exist in the space between two eternities, is the biggest human quest.

When the Dalai Lama was asked what surprised him about humanity the most, he responded, "Man… he lives as if he is never going to die, and then dies having never really lived." I encourage you to look at this statement much like you would look at a diamond, turning it around in your mind's eye, for you will be able to see many meanings and uses for it.

Whether you believe that life is a miracle or it is a mistake, or that life has a purpose or it's empty and meaningless, this section in values will shed a deeper insight on understanding why every so often you experience unexplained emotional flare ups.

Energy in Motion

Values are principles or ideals held in the highest regard by your unconscious mind. If there is such a thing as "soul," values would be the closest thing to it, or to the unique energy that makes you and the purpose for your existence in this particular space and time. Values drive the purpose of your life, and they function like a beacon of light that leads the way. I cannot tell you what your life's purpose is, the same way I cannot tell you what to do with all the time you have on this planet. I can, however, help you find it with quest prompts, much like I have done with my coaching clients.

The quest to either find purpose or fill the time is a personal one. And because you have a unique energy blueprint, and no other being on the planet can be like you, only you can fulfill that purpose.

Much like the 10 commandments etched in stone, values are like the golden rules that shouldn't be broken, but because we are cursed and blessed with free will and forgetfulness, we can break them whenever we want. But precisely because they are held in the highest regard by your unconscious mind, you will likely encounter an emotional flare up every time you cross the line or have veered too far off from your values path. Remember, emotions are the preferred way for your unconscious mind to reach you.

Values are specific to different areas of your life. For example, your top three values for your career might be work ethic, money, and relationships, and your top three values for your family life might be love, respect, and growth. It probably would be in detriment to your marriage if you put money as your top value in your relationship with your spouse, and it would likely be detrimental to your job if you put fun as your number one value in your career. This is the reason why it's useful to observe the values in separate and specific areas of your life.

When I guide my clients into a deeper analysis of values in different areas, I urge them to make note of the reoccurring cluster of values that show up across the board, although in different hierarchies. This is one way that some of them have made great progress at finding their life's purpose. Another method I have worked with was directly eliciting the values for "My Life's Purpose."

There are countless stories of successful businessmen who forfeited their rich lives to wander around the world with nothing but a back pack. To the outer world, they appear to have gone mad, without reason or logic, but to this person's inner world, this was the path that needed to be taken. This is the story of Buddha himself, grown among riches and nobility, leaving all behind to seek his path to enlightenment.

Changing the outer world is one popular way to realign with values, but it is certainly not the only way. You do not need to quit your job, nor leave your spouse, nor become a nomad, to better align with your values and life's purpose.

There is a popular book out there that describes the journey of a traveler who left point A to circle the world in search of point B, only to find that point B was exactly all the way back in point A. I will not tell you what that book is, so that I don't spoil the surprise for you once it's your time to read it.

There is a useful formula in understanding the ripple effect that values have in your life. Knowing it will help you put into perspective the cascade of events you might have been experiencing:

VALUES > BELIEFS > BEHAVIORS (actions) over time = HABITS that shape your REALITY

You will also find it helpful in a personal analysis to understand the following: A belief will be accepted or rejected based on how in line it is with your personal values. Emotions are the compass tool to recalibrate your course of action, and physical evidence is the ultimate proof of having changed your reality. Beliefs are consciously accepted but also subconsciously implanted, and so it is important to make a belief audit once in a while. Habits are an action repeated over time, which is now part of the unconscious competence, and because it has created a deep rooted neural network, it's either going to take a lot of time, effort, and correct repetitions to change that, or it's going to take some reprogramming at the unconscious mind level.

If you want to start to peel this onion with me, check out the free mini course on values, at EnergyinMotionBook.com.

HOW TO TAKE BACK PERSONAL POWER

If you were to go on a road trip across your country, at a bare minimum you would need a vehicle. If you were to jump in it and start driving without any supplies, you would still get somewhere—although I don't know how far—before you either got thirsty or hungry or ran out of gas, but you would definitely at least get somewhere.

But if you had an unlimited flow of the bare minimum resources to fuel yourself and your car, such as water, food, gas, and money, you could keep traveling for years if you wanted.

Since the day a caterpillar hatches, it has one job: to eat as much as it can, as fast as it can; and it starts with its own eggshell. Depending on the species, this gluttonous little fellow outgrows itself about 1,000 times, and if by the law of nature it has eaten enough, it gets to lay eggs and then metamorphose into the angelic version of its species: a butterfly, after having broken itself down inside the cocoon.

When it comes to you or any one person who has made the conscious decision to grow and change into a more purposeful or awakened self, gathering resources is as important as preparing for a road trip—or in the case of the caterpillar, to eat its body weight a thousand times before metamorphosis time.

The most precious resources needed to embrace a personal transformation are time, energy, and money. Any current activities, relationships, or places that you may perceive as wasteful in any degree are regarded as a leakage of energy by your unconscious mind. You would not go driving around knowing that your gas tank was leaking. You would be wasting gas, and in danger of exploding! The same happens with energy leaks.

Take a second right now and, in your mind, name three items in your life that make you feel drained after interacting with them. If I were to mind read, I am sure you might have mentioned your job or a specific person, and maybe the unnecessary time you spend on social media.

There are other areas closer to home that might be hard to consider. To acknowledge that some personal or family aspects are in truth detrimental to us could bring bubbles of conflict and guilt to the surface. This emotional response comes from how we have been programmed as a society. Family always comes first, sometimes even to the detriment of an individual.

Break the mold, allow yourself a space to acknowledge if this is the case, and forgive yourself if you need to do that.

You do not need to beat yourself up for allowing yourself to observe what is already there, and by doing this, you can now move into more creative ways of being, as opposed to reactive ways of feeling. Remember what you learned about shapeshifting. This change has to do with you, not with them.

Acknowledging areas that leak power in your life does not mean that you *have to*, might *want to*, or even *can* eliminate them from your life right now. It simply means to bring to the light of awareness where there is a possibility to create a personal boundary.

The action of creating a personal boundary is very much like casting one of those spells you see the witches do in movies. They draw a circle around themselves, along with different geometrical shapes and arcane symbols, and stand in the center or outside of it. Nothing enters, nothing gets out, and yet they are able to interact with the summoned spirit or demon.

A personal boundary is a conscious decision about how you are going to interact with a person or place, and under what circumstances. Casting a personal boundary means stating the rules of the game and making sure they are followed.

The first boundary that must be explored is a boundary with ourselves, because within it lies the power to be at cause. If you are at cause, you can create and recreate any boundary that you need with the outer world, but if you are not at cause, you are most likely in victim mode, left exposed to the storm of outside circumstances.

Energy is unlimited and replenishable, but time is not. Money comes and goes, and it is the resource that allows you to invest in yourself, to sign up for courses, hire a coach, buy more books, go on a nurturing trip, etc.

Time, money, and energy: Do you have it to give? Do you want to give it? Under what circumstances? Where, when, how, and with whom? Write your own contracts with yourself. You can start simply by casting a boundary on as little as 20 minutes a day, which no one and nothing can touch, other than you. Within those 20 minutes, choose one activity that replenishes your energy and well-being. It can be anything as grounding as going for a foot massage or taking a bubble bath, to the most spiritual undertaking, like writing affirmations for world peace or meditating in silence.

There are no rules; stop buying that story.

I invite you to make your own.

CREATING VIBRATIONAL COHERENCE

Similar attracts similar, and your vibe attracts your tribe. It is the *law of attraction*. Ultimately, the physical reality, the people, places, and objects that surround you are the truest physical evidence of the values, beliefs, decisions, emotions, and other ethereal vibrations you carry inside of you, some of which are conscious and some of which are veiled. The physical reality that surrounds you, your body, your relationships, your job, your income, your house, and your community, ultimately holds the biggest clue to what you carry inside.

Always look to the physical evidence to find clues on areas of opportunity. For example, if you do not have the income you believe you deserve, or the love life you know you want, it is of great use to take the physical reality as a feedback system and become your own reality detective, using some of the techniques you have learned throughout this book, or the resources on my website. Yes, this takes a BIG level of ownership, and it is something to constantly strive for; and there will be moments that where you will hear yourself say, "I refuse to believe I caused this." I know I do this once in a while, and that's okay... I eventually come back when I get fed up with hearing my own stuck story and revisit the opportunities for growth that have presented themselves to me.

The first step to taking back personal power, as you learned in the previous section, is to create personal boundaries, and that might involve cutting cords with any person, place, or thing that you perceive to be a leakage of energy. Once you have taken one action step toward this, you might notice a slight increase of space and energy within you. This will be the perfect incentive for you to continue along this path.

Once you have taken care of the leakages of energy, it is time to nurture and grow your personal power by surrounding yourself with the vibrations of who you plan to become.

For example, if you want to become a writer, and you don't even know where to start, a good idea is to take a journal, or your computer, and hang out at the coffee shop, surrounded by the people who seem to effortlessly be typing away. Trust me, the vibe gets contagious, and you might find yourself inspired to write. I call this *vibrational coherence* which is in line with a possible higher version of yourself.

There are six main categories that can be used to elevate your vibration and create coherence with that of a higher version of yourself.

Below, you will read an insightful introduction into what each of them entail. Grab a notebook and make note of any ideas that come to mind about what you might be inspired to do. Remember, an idea lives in the invisible world, and you make it come to life with actions. The most powerful form of action is inspired action. Look out for a feeling of excitement as you read the descriptions.

Language. It is not only the means by which you grasp the world around you, but also by which you create the world around you. The label you put on a person, object, or situation can change how that person, object, or situation interacts with you, and vice versa. Language is as personal as reality, as universal as humankind, and as vast as the infinite number of word combinations, but is as limited as the word that boxes things. Language is the code of creation. Creating a vibrational match with language has to do with "watching your mouth," as discussed in Chapter 2. Language is created as it leaves your mouth, and so it likely defines you through the ears of other persons. The best way to look for areas of opportunity is to ask the people you trust to describe you. Create a safe space for them, and open your ears and your heart to their feedback. Also, don't be afraid of silence; silence is the empty space that allows the true nature of things to shine through, and a space for the new to enter your life. Noise is unnecessary clutter. Start paying attention to your conversations with others—are they noise, or do they add any form of value?

2. People, places, and things. Surround yourself with that which is in line with the direction of who you want to become. Likeminded people with likeminded interests are great, but you will likely remain the same if you don't broaden your horizons. If you want to continue growing, seek to mingle with people whose energy is ahead of you. This might make you uncomfortable at the beginning, due to the contrast it creates, but soon enough, you will notice how you start moving faster toward a higher version of yourself. Hang around places that make you feel the feelings you want to feel, and only pursue the objects that function as anchors toward your goals. An anchor is something that functions as a reminder of your goal or desire, or a standard that you hold dear to your heart. For

Energy in Motion

example, a wedding ring is an anchor to the love and values you hold dear with your partner. Much like noise, unnecessary things are clutter that might serve to erroneously fill a void. Decluttering literally and metaphorically creates an empty space for new and better things to enter your life.

3. *Food* is the most intimate relationship between your body and the outer world. Food enters the body an average of three times a day. Take a moment to let the following realization sink in: By choosing what you eat, you open the gateway for an item from the outer world into your inner world, and allow it become part of you. This is why what you choose to eat can be the fastest way to heal yourself or poison yourself. The reality is that your unconscious mind has been bombarded by subliminal messages from the media; and today, you and I, and most people on this planet, are confused as to what a healthy human diet should look and feel like. Also, everybody is a planet in its own right, with its own ecosystem of microbes, and that is why the same healthy diet will give two people very different results. Ultimately, your physical body does not lie, and it will always give you the harsh truth—if it aches constantly, gets sick often, and carries unwanted weight, what is your body telling you? Remember that P.A.I.N. is an acronym for: *pay attention in the now.*

4. *Movement,* much like food, is a personal experience. That is why not everybody likes yoga, and not everybody likes going to the gym. Some people love dancing, and others prefer hiking. The right type of movement is lotion for your body and boosts you with energy; the wrong type of movement for a person is usually painful or boring. Movement is a multidimensional experience. It comes in different wavelengths: slow, medium, fast, and explosive; and it can be intertwined with different intentions: strength training, movement meditation, sexy dancing, etc. The best advice I can give you is to experience different types of movements, and also different teachers

within the same discipline, and find which one gives you the *bliss point*. You will know you have tapped into the bliss point if you feel any of the following, or a combination of: joy, grounding, peace, a mental or physical boost, an intimate sense of self, being nurtured, becoming empowered, and other blissful variations of your higher self.

5. *Music* is a multilayered experience of tones, beats, words, sounds, and emotions, just to name a few of those complex layers. When you are listening to music, your heart naturally gravitates toward a vibrational coherence with the song you are listening to. Your heart rate rises by a few beats per minute when you listen to angry or uplifting music, and it lowers a few beats per minute to match calming or meditational songs. Isn't that amazing! Your heart-self regulates to create a vibrational coherence with sound. This is why it is important that you pay attention to the physiological effect that music has on you, and use it consciously to create the emotional states you desire, not to feed those you don't. The words contained in songs function as subliminal messages to your unconscious mind. It tends to take everything personally, so if you find yourself cursing a little too much all of a sudden, you might want to pay attention to what music they are playing at your gym, just to name an example.

6. *Posture.* Great posture requires mindfulness. Becoming aware of your posture is like becoming aware of obscure aspects of your consciousness. But among many reasons, when it comes to vibrational coherence, the way you hold your body can elevate or depress your vibration. Do this simple exercise, wherever you are: Round your back, slouch your shoulders, and make the saddest or angriest face you can make. Sit with it for a couple of minutes and make note of how it makes you feel. Now stand up; stand with your feet slightly wider than hip-width apart, put your hands on your hips, raise your chest and your eyes to about 75 degrees, and smile.

Energy in Motion

Hold this *superhero pose* for a couple of minutes, and notice how it makes you feel—emotionally, physically, mentally, and any other aspects of this experience. The truth is that your mind affects your posture (body), but it can also happen in reverse!

I could write a whole book on each of these categories. They are fascinating journeys to explore. I have started by creating more online resources for you to dive deeper into your category of choice. Visit my website for more information.

In the meantime, if you were able to find even one idea that inspires you to make a change in any of these six areas, go ahead and take the first step. Action is the embodiment of *Energy in Motion*. You have traveled the introductory journey of what it means to *unleash your mind*, and so it is time for you to *take one small action now that can change the course of your future*.

You will find the instructions of what that is, in the next and last section of this book.

EXERCISE YOUR POWER TO CREATE

To an artist, an architect, and a writer, there is nothing more daunting and also exciting than an empty page or canvas staring back at them. That blank space is full of infinite possibilities. Committing to one of them means to eliminate all others. Committing to one of those possibilities also means taking ownership of the power to create.

Ever since you came into this world, you were told how to behave, what to do, and who you needed to be, by your parents, by your teachers, by the community you were a part of, by the government, etc. What no one ever told you is that if you want, you have the power to reshape who you are and the world around you. How could they have known, when they cannot possibly know all the unique traits and gifts that make you who you are. Sadly, some of them don't even know who they are either.

In taking ownership of this revelation, it means that you and you alone can write the map for the next stage of your life, however you define it to be. It takes courage—trust me, I know.

The next page is an empty page for you to practice what it means to step into your creator power. Putting pen to paper is the first step to taking something from the invisible world and manifesting it in the physical world. That is why a lot of books and coaches use writing as part of their curriculums. It is a manifesting tool.

You get to be the architect now. You get to be the artist, or the writer of this new chapter. Use the following questions as writing prompts:

What do you want, or where do you want to go? This represents the source of motion, the ignition key.

Why do you want it? This represents the fuel. Use emotion and make it passionate; make it good and make it so powerful that it fuels you even through the dark days and right until the end. Your "why" is the energy that will infuse your actions with life.

How can you achieve that, or who do you need to reach out to for help, or for coaching or guidance? This is the map of where you are going. If you know how, the only thing you need to do is take the first step and see what happens. If you have no idea how to get to where you want to be, start looking for the resource or the person that can guide you. You don't need to do it all by yourself.

You might want to, but you don't need to. Just try something different for once.

How long are you giving yourself to play this game like it is the only one that matters, or by when do you need this completed by? This has to do with energy management. The feeling of working toward a goal for too long can possibly deplete you. Despite how powerful you are, it is okay to be human and to choose a period of time to give it your all, and choose a period to rest, be lazy, or cut yourself some slack. This was a key step for me to be able to finish this book.

If you finish this quest, I invite you to share it with me. I will be delighted to know of the progress you have made, and I might have a surprise to share with you. Take a picture of your blank page when it is no longer blank, and send it to alediazme@gmail.com, or if you are ready to share your statement with the world, place it on Instagram, Facebook, or other social media of your choice, with the hash tag:

#EnergyInMotionBookBlankPage

Step into your creator power, and have fun while you are at it. After all, this is you, and only you, creating possibilities in your life.

www.EnergyInMotionBook.com

THIS IS MY BLANK PAGE

ABOUT THE AUTHOR

Alejandra Díaz Mercado is originally from Mexico City and currently resides in Burlington, ON, Canada. She has integrated more than 10 years of her work as a personal trainer, fascial stretch therapist, and neuro-linguistic master practitioner, and art practice, into the creation of this book.

She holds both an in-person and an online practice, with individuals and groups. Her work is dedicated to guiding you in understanding the use and purpose of your body, your mind, and your emotions as vehicles of motion to transform the world around you.

With a true entrepreneurial spirit looking to inspire on a larger scale, she has partnered up with companies of international presence, dedicated to bringing an experience of growth through health, fitness, and wellness, both as a presenter and as a kinetic artist.

She is looking to partner up with visionaries to create more awakenings and emotional experiences that will move the audience to self-empowerment and a better world.

Learn what energy in motion means in your own world. To connect with the author for rates, availability, and any other inquiries, she can be reached at:

alediazme@gmail.com

For learning more about current programs and projects connected to Energy in Motion, visit:

www.EnergyInMotionBook.com

Finally, if you have been moved by the content of *Energy in Motion, How to Unleash Your Mind and Take Action Now,* be a source of energy in someone else's life, and move it into their hands. Know that your action is a pebble in a pond, which creates expansive waves with far-reaching consequences tied to the awakening of human consciousness. You are a vehicle with the potential to change this world.

Manufactured by Amazon.ca
Bolton, ON